50 Proven Ways to Make Passive Income Online & Remotely

By Chris Friesing

Introduction

Many think that living comfortably (or at least making ends meet) involves slaving away in the office and doing overtime work whenever there's a chance. Well, while that belief might have been true a decade ago, it definitely doesn't apply to these modern times. With the sheer pace at which technology evolves, particularly in the online world, countless new opportunities have emerged.

In this book, you will discover fifty of the best ways of generating income through the web. Regardless of your interests and skill, you'll find something in here that's right for you. Also, you won't be disappointed regardless of your earning preferences, since we have listed passive, semi-passive, and active earning opportunities.

Simply put, with this book, you'll finally have the chance to enter a new world – one which gives you full control of your financial goals and working hours. Once you're ready, head on to the first chapter to begin your search for that perfect modern moneymaking pursuit.

Table of Contents

50 PROVEN WAYS TO MAKE PASSIVE INCOME ONLINE & REMOTELY — 1

INTRODUCTION — 3

CHAPTER 1: EARNING THROUGH THE WEB — 7

CHAPTER 2: AMAZON FBA — 11

CHAPTER 3: MERCH BY AMAZON — 13

CHAPTER 4: AMAZON KINDLE — 15

CHAPTER 5: EBAY — 18

CHAPTER 6: ETSY — 21

CHAPTER 7: PINTEREST — 24

CHAPTER 8: FACEBOOK — 26

CHAPTER 9: AFFILIATE MARKETING THROUGH BLOGGING — 28

CHAPTER 10: INSTAGRAM — 32

CHAPTER 11: TWITTER — 35

CHAPTER 12: GOOGLE PLUS — 38

CHAPTER 13: LINKEDIN — 41

CHAPTER 14: YOUTUBE — 44

CHAPTER 15: DAY TRADING (FX AND STOCKS) — 47

CHAPTER 16: E-BOOKS   49

CHAPTER 17: AUDIO BOOKS   52

CHAPTER 18: APPS   54

CHAPTER 19: E-MAIL MARKETING   57

CHAPTER 20: STOCK PHOTOS   60

CHAPTER 21: AIRBNB   63

CHAPTER 22: SHOPIFY   66

CHAPTER 23: ANSWERING PROFESSIONAL QUESTIONS   68

CHAPTER 24: ONLINE COURSES   70

CHAPTER 25: VIRTUAL ASSISTANT   73

CHAPTER 26: ONLINE TEACHER/TUTOR   75

CHAPTER 27: WEB DESIGN   77

CHAPTER 28: ARTICLE WRITING   79

CHAPTER 29: GRAPHIC DESIGN   84

CHAPTER 30: ONLINE SURVEYS   86

CHAPTER 31: SWAGBUCKS   89

CHAPTER 32: WEBSITE TESTING   93

CHAPTER 33: PRODUCT REVIEW   96

CHAPTER 34: DATA ENTRY   98

CHAPTER 35: ONLINE TRAVEL AGENT   101

CHAPTER 36: ONLINE GAMES   103

CHAPTER 37: SEARCH ENGINES   106

CHAPTER 38: ONLINE JUROR   108

CHAPTER 39: FREELANCE TRANSCRIPTION   111

CHAPTER 40: RENT STUFF ONLINE   113

CHAPTER 41: PEER-TO-PEER LENDING   114

CHAPTER 42: CASH BACK, GIFT CARDS, AND REBATES   117

CHAPTER 43: JUNK MAIL   119

CHAPTER 44: NO-RISK MATCHED BETTING   121

CHAPTER 45: CLICKWORKER   123

CHAPTER 46: FIVERR   124

CHAPTER 47: MUSIC REVIEW   128

CHAPTER 48: SELLING NOTES AND LESSON PLANS   131

CHAPTER 49: BUY AND SELL DOMAIN NAMES 133

CHAPTER 50: MULTILEVEL MARKETING   136

CHAPTER 51: ONLINE TRANSLATOR   138

CONCLUSION   140

Chapter 1: Earning through the Web

There's a change in the moneymaking landscape as the world becomes more and more reliant on the internet. Many conventional jobs are becoming obsolete as society shifts towards the digital. Consider the number of employees in the newspaper industry. In the 1990s, the US Bureau of Statistics identified almost 500,000 individuals involved in the trade. Just 13 years later (which coincides with the advent of the internet), the total went down to 200,000.

It's not surprising at all that some think the newspaper industry won't last much longer, given that it has been completely overtaken by digital media in terms of readership. While the world's continuing transition towards the internet might put many conventional earning opportunities in jeopardy, it's also creating a myriad of new ways to generate income – and there's a lot in store for those willing to give these a try, and we're not just talking about financial gains.

Why Should You Aim to Earn Online?

If you are fed up with your day job and you have had enough of your boss and co-workers, perhaps it is time to quit and start earning online. Of course, you're free to pursue both a day job and one of the modern opportunities that will be discussed in the next chapters, especially if you're still searching for that ideal moneymaking pursuit. If you're still hesitant to try something new though, you should probably think of these potential advantages in generating income online:

You can be your own boss.

Gone are the days when you have to bend backwards just to please someone else – your boss! When you become your boss, you no longer have to abide by the rules of a company. You get to decide when you want to work or when you wish to take a break. No one would be there to breathe down your neck and bark orders at you all day long. You are free to make your own work schedule and decide when to take a vacation.

You do not have to work in an office.

You can work at home or practically anywhere, which means more convenience and comfort on your part. You do not have to wear corporate attire, so you'll enjoy more savings on clothing. You can even work while in your pajamas, unless you need to make a video call during which you should at least put on a decent shirt with a collar. Staying at home also means more peace of mind and relaxation. If you are an introvert and you prefer to work alone, having no overly chatty co-workers can be such a breath of fresh air.

You can have more time for your family and yourself.

Busy people with busy schedules rarely have time for family, friends, and even themselves. When you start working at home, you will realize how valuable your time is. Working at home allows you to take care of your children and watch them grow. You can also sleep and eat better, as well as pamper yourself. Home-based work opportunities give you benefits that major companies cannot offer, such as flexible work schedules.

You can continue and/or further your education.

Many online pursuits do not require a high level of education, only specific skill sets. If you possess the right skills, you can earn even if you do not have a bachelor's or master's degree.

Since you have a flexible work schedule and you can work from anywhere, you can work and study at the same time.

You can have an unlimited earning potential.

With a day job, you earn a fixed amount. If you want to earn more money, you have to work overtime or work a second shift. With an online moneymaking opportunity, however, you can earn as much money as possible. When you put in more time and effort, the amount of money you earn can double or triple.

You have a lot of pursuits to choose from.

The web offers numerous ways of making money. If you're the kind who prefers not to be too involved in work on a daily basis, you'll be glad to know that there are various passive and semi-passive income opportunities online. You could rent out your property with the help of online hubs, and you could also make money through well-placed advertisements. Writing an eBook, taking stock photos, and even making applications are also good options – if you have the right skills.

If, on the other hand, you want to make active income, you still won't run out of choices. Numerous people are currently working online as graphic designers, virtual assistants, and data entry specialists. Well, there are other unorthodox options such as playing games and being part of an online jury. As you read this book, you will realize that you won't really have a problem finding a gig – it's much more likely that you will end up overwhelmed by the sheer number and variety of opportunities available to you.

You see, it is not that difficult to work from home. The startup costs are minimal, so you do not have to spend a lot of money. In most cases, all you need is a computer with an Internet connection. Some jobs require you to have additional tools and equipment such as a headset or a microphone, though.

The benefits are great, but many people still remain skeptical. With the state of the economy and the rising prices of goods and commodities, most people do not want to take risks. They want to feel safe and secure, which is why they stick with their day jobs.

While it is true that you will not enjoy the perks of having an insurance policy issued by a company or a regular paycheck every month, the perks and privileges to be had are still plenty. At first, it can be overwhelming and intimidating, but you should not worry because you will eventually get the hang of it. In due time, you will learn the ropes of working an online job and earning good income.

In the succeeding chapters, you will learn about the top 50 online money making opportunities. You should learn about them and follow the tips given in this book so that you can enjoy the benefits of being financially independent.

Chapter 2: Amazon FBA

Amazon.com, one of the most well-known online retailers in the world, offers a moneymaking opportunity for people seeking to earn a passive income. This service is known as Fulfillment By Amazon or FBA. It handles the backend operations of third-party sellers, such as storage, customer service, and fulfillment.

When you become a third-party seller, you can ship your inventory to Amazon. It will then manage the whole backend fulfillment of your items once they are ordered and paid for. It is typical for third-party sellers who ship their goods via Amazon to benefit from a bigger customer base and a much faster delivery time.

About 40% of the unit sales of Amazon are attributed to third-party sellers. In 2013, they generated over $17 billion. Amazon also states that 73% of their survey participants reported a 20% increase in their unit sales after joining Fulfillment By Amazon.

Third-party sellers become attracted to FBA because they know that Amazon is an expert when it comes to logistics. They are aware of its great logistics infrastructure, which makes it possible to efficiently pick, pack, and ship orders. In addition, products over $35 are eligible for free two-day shipping. Sellers are also confident with the reliable returns policies and customer service of Amazon.

Then again, even though it sounds great to join Fulfillment By Amazon, you still have to do your own research beforehand, just so you can be certain of what you are getting yourself into.

For instance, some sellers report the comingling of merchandise in the program. You know that Amazon has different centers all over the country. This allows them to ship products from the nearest location. So, if a buyer from Nevada buys an item from a third-party seller from Florida, Amazon will give credit to the seller in Florida but will give the buyer an item from California, since it is nearer.

Buyers may have no problem with this setup, but it can be quite troublesome for sellers. If you are the seller, it would be difficult for you to control the quality of the product. This can cause you to gain negative reviews from buyers, or even face legal liabilities.

Aside from this, you may also have issues with sales tax compliance. Once the company receives the items, it starts to ship them to different facilities. As a seller, you will not be provided with the information as to where your goods are going to be sent to. You will not even know about the warehouses. So, it will be difficult for you to register for your sales tax compliance. You may also experience liability issues.

Furthermore, you have to be prepared for competitive pressures. As you know, Amazon has a wide variety of products. It also keeps track of its sales as well as adjusts their sourced merchandise. Because of this, you may experience problems with revenue cuts when Amazon starts to directly compete with you.

Nevertheless, in spite of the abovementioned drawbacks, you may still find it rewarding to be part of Fulfillment By Amazon. Sellers like the fact that the company offers unparalleled logistics and they have a huge customer base. If you are running a startup business, the exposure you get from Amazon can do wonders for your sales.

Chapter 3: Merch by Amazon

Merch is another moneymaking opportunity from Amazon. It is relatively new, but it has already convinced a lot of people to join. It is a self-service program that was specifically created to help u boost your revenues from sales of branded shirts. You get to design t-shirts and unleash your creativity. You can leave the production, selling, and shipping to Amazon. You can even use pre-made templates from Amazon, but it is still better if you can use art, icons, or logos from your game to promote your brand.

The great thing about Merch is that you will not waste money. It has a print on demand policy, so you do not have to worry about out of pocket expenses and inventories. You can simply sell shirts by order. There is no need for you to stock a bunch of shirts and wait for customers to order all of them. For each one of these shirts sold, you get to earn a royalty, which depends on your list price and Amazon's listing fee and cost. So, the more shirts you sell, the more money you make. You can use Amazon's calculator to help you set your list price and determine how much royalty you can earn for every shirt.

Even better, it is so easy to start your business. All you have to do is set up an account at Merch by Amazon. Then, you have to upload your t-shirt artwork and click on the submit button. Amazon would take care of everything else for you. So, you can sit back and relax. After just a few hours, you can expect your personally designed shirts to be available already. You can then sell your merchandise online for people from different parts of the world to see.

A lot of developers are delighted with Merch by Amazon because it allows them to poll their Facebook fans and pique their minds with regard to ideas for t-shirt designs. The entire process is also quick and easy. You can start on a Monday and finish on a Wednesday. With such a short timeframe like that, you can produce and sell as many shirts as you want, allowing you to have an unlimited earning potential.

You can promote your custom shirts online and in-game, including on iOS, Android, and Fire OS versions of games with help from Amazon Mobile Ads. The Amazon Mobile Ads API is cross-platform and allows you to include in-app shirt promotions to your applications as house ads. Promoting your merchandise through ads allow you to capture the attention of players whom you can turn into buyers and even advocates of your game. Keeping your game players happy and satisfied is essential for business success.

Chapter 4: Amazon Kindle

Amazon does not only offer a lot of goods, but it also offers a wide range of moneymaking opportunities. Aside from FBA and Merch, you can also make money through Amazon Kindle. In essence, you can earn a passive income by creating electronic books or e-books for Kindle.

As an author, you can either get 70% or 35% royalty on the e-book price. This may not seem like a lot, but if you create and sell tons of e-books on Amazon, you can earn a pretty decent sum of money. See to it that you check out the pricing page so that you can be guided accordingly with regard to payments.

If you want to boost your earning potential through your Kindle books, you have to turn your readers into subscribers. Keep in mind that people who purchase e-books on Amazon Kindle are customers. Hence, they are your perfect choice for email subscribers. If you want to lure them, you have to offer them a gift or a bonus at the end and beginning parts of your books. People are generally fond of gifts and freebies, so giving them something extra would entice them and ignite their interest.

This gift or bonus has to lead to a report connected to your e-book subject. Of course, the two topics have to be related to make sure that the customer is getting more of what he or she paid for. In other words, you need to provide added value to what is already discussed in your e-book.

For example, you can offer a copy of your "Stock Market Tips" book for free as well as a spot on your early bird list for your "Beginner's Guide to Investing" report. You have to provide your readers with incentives so that they will be encouraged to join your mailing list and try your brand.

See to it that you also provide links to Money Pages or the spots on your website wherein visitors can find added content as well as obtain information with regard to earning opportunities. In other words, you have to include links to pages that contain relevant content so that you can earn more money.

Visitors who came to your site in search of ways to make cash may also be interested in creating their own website. If this is the case, you can reference pages in which people can find out how to set up their own websites. You can place these reference pages at the beginning of your books.

Furthermore, you can add affiliate links to your products. You have to be extra careful with this method, however. You must know how to use the right amount of links. If you use too many links, your visitors might give you negative reviews. It is always best to be honest with your visitors too. You have to tell them about your affiliate links so that they will not feel deceived.

Then again, the real key to earning money online via Amazon Kindle is to gain a high ranking in the search engines, such as Google, for keywords that are highly in demand. Even though Amazon is already popular all over the world, adding backlinks to your page can still do wonders for your rankings. You may have to be creative in finding ways to add backlinks if your backlinking tool does not link Amazon pages.

One of the best things about the Internet is that you can self-publish your own book and sell it. Gone are the days when you solely have to rely on major publishers to get your work printed out. Today, you can sell soft copies of your work in the form of e-books. It is easy, convenient, and cost-effective. You can earn more money from Amazon Kindle if you publish a new book on a monthly basis.

Chapter 5: eBay

Without a doubt, eBay is one of the most successful e-commerce companies worldwide. It is actually the biggest online marketplace today. It offers consumer-to-consumer and business-to-consumer sales services. With over 97 million users, you can expect thousands of goods to be sold every day. So, if you need anything, you can turn to eBay to look for it.

Keep in mind that eBay is not just a place you go to if you want to sell old clothes and stuff. You can make it your fulltime job. A lot of sellers actually depend on it for a living, although there are also plenty of part-time sellers there. Being an eBay seller is pretty simple. You just have to sign up. Signing up is free of charge, but you have to pay certain fees the moment you start selling your merchandise.

In essence, there are several ways on how you can sell on eBay: auction, buy it now, best offer, and multi-quantity.

The auction format allows you to give your item to the highest bidder. This format is ideal if your items are currently in high demand. You can expect tons of people to bid on them. You get to control your pricing as well as the duration of your auction. You can hold your action for as long as you want.

Experts recommend holding your auction for more than a week. According to researchers at the University of Michigan as well as the University of Arizona, holding an auction for five days gives you the same result as holding it for just three days. On the other hand, holding an auction for at least seven days gives you an added twenty to forty percent on bids.

In addition, it is not advisable to end an auction during the "happy hour" or the time when many other sellers compete for customers. Researchers at the University of Pennsylvania found that eBay sellers who end their auctions during the "happy hour" become ten percent less likely to make a sale. This is why it is not a good idea to leave the site during peak hours.

The Buy It Now format is ideal for eBay sellers who want to earn money quickly and set fixed prices for their merchandise. This format prompts customers to order and pay for an item as soon as possible. However, before you go with this format, you have to make sure that you know the exact market prices of your merchandise. A good rule of thumb is to research how much they cost in offline and other online stores. Being aware of how much goods cost lets you set your prices accordingly and stay competitive.

If you go with the Buy It Now format, you can sell your items before your reserved price is met and even before the auction starts. The moment a customer clicks on your item, it is considered sold. However, you also have to make sure that you meet the criteria before you decide to choose this format. For example, if you want to go with Fixed Price for your listing, see to it that your feedback rating is at least 30. You also have to choose PayPal as your method of payment.

If it is okay for you to haggle, you can choose the Best Offer format. It allows your customers to give you a price, which you can either accept or reject. This format, however, is only valid for a maximum of forty-eight hours. It is also binding. Hence, you have to weigh the pros and cons before you finally settle for a specific price and accept a customer's offer for your merchandise.

Then, there is the multi-quantity format, which is recommended if you have two or more items of the same kind. You can offer these items for a discounted price. For example, if you have an item that you sell for $25 per piece, you can offer four pieces for only $80. This would encourage customers who want to save money or buy in bulk.

Chapter 6: Etsy

Etsy, the handmade equivalent of eBay, is also a highly popular e-commerce website with millions of sellers and buyers from different parts of the world. If you are into making handmade products, you can sell your stuff on the site. Etsy also offers vintage items, craft supplies, art, jewelry, toys, food, bath items, and cosmetics among others. They even have digital items that customers can download such as patterns, photographs, and audio files.

Etsy is ideal for people who want to earn on the web. Just like eBay, it has a strong reputation and a huge following. Each day, tons of customers go to the site to search for items. So, if your items are interesting, useful, and reasonably priced, you can guarantee sales and positive feedback.

Etsy has a user-friendly interface, which makes it appealing to everyone, including those who are not that tech savvy. Customers can easily and quickly find what they are looking for. As a seller, you will not have a hard time listing your items. You can conveniently choose your headers, prices, and keywords. You can also upload photos and descriptions with ease.

In case you have a question with regard to the selling policies of the site, you can contact customer support as well as talk to other sellers. Etsy is not just an e-commerce website. It is a community where sellers come together to discuss things and help one another.

You will also be pleased to find out that the fees of Etsy are much lower than those of eBay. So, you can save more money selling from this site. When you sign up with eBay, you are required to pay $0.20 for every listing. This listing is good for thirty days at most.

On the other hand, when you sign up with Etsy, your $0.20 listing can last for a hundred and twenty days – that is roughly equivalent to four months! On Etsy, you also only have to pay for the items that you include in your listings. Moreover, transaction fees are lower on Etsy. The costs are 3.5% lower than that of eBay.

Etsy is highly recommended for first-time sellers who wish to test the waters first and hone their marketing skills. The site is already established, so there is no more need to start from scratch. This saves new sellers time, money, and energy since they are already provided with a platform that they can use to find out if they can make a living from online selling.

If you are a new seller, all you have to do is sign up and create an account. Then, you can upload your items and start selling to make money. You will find a variety of social buttons on Etsy. You can use these buttons to further increase your store's popularity and attract more customers. Your customers can provide you with valuable feedback. You can even gain feedback before you sell your items. Keep in mind that a lot of customers rely on the comments and feedback sections to check the reliability and reputation of the seller. This is why you need to do your best to gain positive feedback if you want to keep getting customers.

Don't forget to use relevant tags for your merchandise. Search engine optimization or SEO is crucial in online marketing. You have to use the right keywords and key phrases so that customers can easily locate your store. It is not recommended to use generic tags. As much as possible, you have to use tags that describe your items. You must also include clear and accurate photos, as well as appropriate descriptions.

Chapter 7: Pinterest

Pinterest has more than seventy million users and receives more than two billion page views every month. With its massive popularity among users, you can rest assured that its moneymaking opportunities are massive too. In fact, there are a variety of ways on how you can make money from Pinterest.

For starters, you can build an audience while doing what you love and turn your fans into customers. You can literally earn passive income just by pursuing your passion. For example, if you are into staying fit and healthy, you can inspire people who want to be just like you. You can create an account on Pinterest and upload boards that will satisfy your audience. You can upload photos of yourself exercising or the kind of food that you eat to stay fit. Once you gain enough followers, you can create an email listing. Marketers usually contact Pinterest users with several thousand followers or more.

You can also be the one to approach companies. You can ask them to sponsor you in return for promoting their brand. Still using the example given above, you can target companies that are related to health and fitness. For instance, you can go for firms that manufacture sports drinks or sell gym equipment. You can promote what they sell on your Pinterest account since your followers are mainly health and fitness enthusiasts.

A lot of companies are in search of affiliates who are willing to promote their brand in exchange for a commission on sales. So, you can also be an affiliate marketer on Pinterest. You can promote products and services on your boards. Just make sure that you include the affiliate links. You can use URL-shortening services to manage links. They also allow you to track boards and pins for clicks. However, you have to be careful with spamming. Do not be a spammer if you do not want to get banned from Pinterest.

Because you are on the Internet, you have to use search engine optimization effectively. You want users to find your boards and pins. You can incorporate keywords and key phrases on your profile, which consists of two hundred characters. You can also include keywords on your pins, which consists of five hundred characters each. See to it that you sound natural when you use the keywords. Otherwise, your followers will think that you are spamming them.

Another way to make money on Pinterest is through contests. People like to win items and get freebies. You can attract more followers if you hold contests and promise them a gift certificate or some of your items as rewards. Contests are great for engaging customers, but you have to make sure that you abide by Pinterest's guidelines.

In addition, you can create online courses and e-books about Pinterest strategies. This allows you to share your knowledge regarding the moneymaking opportunities on Pinterest, build a following and a network, and earn a passive income all at the same time. You can promote your work on Pinterest by uploading photos and excerpts from your books.

Chapter 8: Facebook

Facebook is a massive and highly influential social media platform with millions of users from different parts of the world. Nearly everyone has a Facebook account. This allows you to interact and communicate with family, friends, colleagues, and even random strangers online. With this being said, you can count on Facebook to be an excellent platform for online marketing.

Affiliate marketing is actually a very common way to make money on Facebook. However, you need to sign up with an affiliate first. Then, you can start promoting their products or services by means of Facebook ads. Each time a user from your page lands on the affiliate merchant's site, you earn a commission. The more visitors your affiliate merchant's site gets, the more money you make.

This is why you have to attract a lot of potential customers. You can create a fan page that appeals to Facebook users. Make sure that you post updates on a regular basis to keep them interested. You should also encourage them to like, share, and comment on the posts. You can even use content that people can make viral, such as images or videos.

Aside from affiliate marketing, you can also make money on Facebook by selling. You can endorse products or services for free. This beats paying for print, radio, and TV ads. You can simply create a fan page and post your merchandise there. You can also include links that redirect users to your online store. There is practically no limit to what you can sell on Facebook. You can promote artwork, digital media, beauty products, gym equipment, spa services, books, music, etc.

You can even use your personal account to advertise your goods. You can share posts from your fan page so that your

Facebook friends will see what you have to offer. If you are using Facebook as a selling platform, you can communicate with your customers via comments or personal messages. Since Facebook does not really have a payment system, you can use online banking, wire transfer, or PayPal as payment method.

Furthermore, you can design and develop applications and then market them on Facebook. These apps are going to be downloaded by customers and installed on their devices, such as computers and smartphones. You can create apps for a variety of purposes, such as gaming, organizing, finance, tracking, and communicating. Your app can be something that makes stock market predictions, tracks to-do lists, or provides trivia. Whatever it is, see to it that the general public would love it.

Apps that are fun and functional really do well on the market. Then again, if you do not possess enough technical skills, you can leave the programming job to someone else. You can hire programmers and developers to create apps for you. Java and PHP are most commonly used to create apps for Facebook, but you can also look into other programming languages.

To test the effectiveness and marketability of your newly developed app, you can release a trial version. You can offer it to users for free, but make sure to encourage them to leave a feedback. If your potential customers liked your app, you can go ahead and release the full version. Apps are actually great moneymaking opportunities. You can earn hundreds of thousands of dollars, and even millions, from creating apps.

Chapter 9: Affiliate Marketing through Blogging

Blogging is an excellent way to talk about your ideas, experiences, and other interesting things. You can even use your blog as an online diary or journal and talk about details from your personal life. You can include pictures, music, and videos for added effect.

Since blogs are easily accessible on the Internet, you can attract the attention of millions of people from different parts of the world. You can take advantage of the traffic you generate to make money and even convert your readers and followers into customers.

You can incorporate affiliate marketing with blogging. Affiliate marketing is when you team up with an online merchant and get paid for endorsing the online merchant's products or services. You earn either a fixed amount or a commission. You have to put ads on your blogs. When your visitors click on these ads, they would be directed to the online store or page of the online merchant.

The following are highly suggested ways on how you can earn a passive income through blogging and affiliate marketing:

1. Generate traffic

    Online income-generation opportunities are mostly about the traffic. This is especially true for affiliate marketing and blogging. It does not matter how interesting or informative your blog is, if you cannot generate sufficient traffic you will not earn money.

    Search engine optimization is effective in generating traffic. Users typically use search engines to find what they need. If your blog appears at the top of the search results, you have a better chance of getting good traffic than other websites.

To make the most of search engine optimization, you must use keywords and key phrases that online users use. You should also go for the ones without much competition. Experts recommend doing research on the most popular keywords and then optimizing your blog to target them.

See to it that your blog loads fast. Keep in mind that visitors tend to get impatient with websites that load slowly. If your blog is slow to load, your visitors may leave before you even get a chance to show them your blog's content.

Refrain from using link spams because they are not helpful. They will not make your blog rank highly on the search engines. In fact, they may even hurt your ranking. Once the search engines detect spam on your blog, they might block your website.

Of course, you should only use relevant content. You also have to be specific to avoid losing potential sales. Make it a point to provide useful, helpful, and interesting content that readers are most likely to share on social media.

2. Use social media platforms.

Speaking of social media, Facebook and Twitter are among the currently popular social media platforms that you can use to promote your blog. You can also use Instagram, Pinterest, and Google Plus. Social media networks are everywhere, and nearly everyone has an account. You can take advantage of social media interaction to earn money. In Facebook, for instance, you can create a fan page and post videos, sound clips, images, and articles that would appeal to your target audience.

In addition, you can buy ads if you want to target a specific demographic. Do not forget to use high quality images, compelling headlines, and a strong call to action. Social media platforms have millions of users. Surely, you will find people who are also interested in your interests. Just keep giving them what they want and you will be able to keep them. Remember that you can gain more followers if you post good content. The more users share and pass them around, the more viral your posts will be.

3. Outsource your content.

Blogging can be fun and exciting, as well as stress relieving. Even better, it can be a source of passive or semi-passive income. Since you are the author of your own posts, you have to make sure that you remain consistent all throughout your blog. You may outsource some of your content, however, to save time and energy. There are plenty of images, videos, articles, and other forms of media that you can find online. You may hire someone else to write your notes. You may also feature other bloggers on your blog.

4. Use an auto responder to automate your sales.

You have to keep in mind that list building and e-mail marketing are highly profitable. So, you must take them seriously. Once you get the email addresses of your readers, you have to refrain from sending spam messages. Remember that nobody likes spam in their inbox. If you send them spam, even just once, they might lose their trust in you completely and never read your messages again. This is why you have to choose your emails carefully. You should also know the right time to email them.

To manage your emails more effectively, you can use an auto responder. You can also use incentives, such as info-products to grab the attention of your blog's visitors. Once they confirm their subscription, your auto responder will start sending emails. Make sure that you have an equal amount of promotional and informative messages in your auto responder. This way, your readers will not think that you are all about marketing your blog. This will allow you to build a good relationship with them.

5. Work with a community manager.

Another way to save time is to work with a community manager. As you know, moderating comments and managing social media accounts can take so much of your valuable time. With a community manager, you can easily engage with your target audience, come up with interesting social media content, and create reports that show how much your returns on investments are. Make sure that you hire a community manager who knows how to make a business grow.

Chapter 10: Instagram

Unlike Facebook and Twitter, Instagram is solely for photos and video clips. So, if you like to take pictures, you can turn to Instagram to earn a passive income. You can license your pictures to companies that use online pictures for branding.

For instance, you can go to Foap, which is a pretty well known photography marketplace online. Signing up is free and easy. Once you have an account, you can start building your profile and portfolio. The better your portfolio is, the more buyers you will attract. You can check out "Missions" for company-paid projects. All you have to do is give them what they want to earn money.

The projects at Missions start with $100, but you have to have really good pictures to stand out from your competitors. Of course, the companies would go with someone who produces high quality, interesting, and unique photos that perfectly match what they are searching for,

There is no need for you to gain a following. You can start making money from your Instagram account immediately. Every photo costs $10, but Foap would take half of what you earn. So, if you want to make a decent amount of money, you should sell more photos. Your payments will be sent to you via PayPal. You can also check out the portfolios of other users, follow their feeds, and provide them with feedback.

Moreover, you can make money from Instagram by teaming up with major brands and becoming an influencer with sponsored posts. An influencer is a person who has a positive reputation online and has a huge following. Their followers consider them as experts, tastemakers, and trendsetters. Their opinions are highly valued by the masses. This is why major companies take advantage of these influencers' popularity for the benefit of their own brand.

You can directly contact the marketing department of various companies. You can also apply at The Mobile Media Lab, which is a creative agency that focuses on bringing advertisers and influencers together. When you get selected to promote a brand, you can earn hundreds or even thousands of dollars for just one post.

You can really earn a lot of money from companies and brands that promote clothes, shoes, accessories, gym equipment, and food among others. According to a survey of five thousand influencers, they mostly charge $200 to $400 for every post. You can also get other deals such as free products and/or services, gifts, and exposure.

Then again, you have to take note that it is not merely the reach and size of your Instagram account that matter when it comes to getting the attention of major companies. Your trustworthiness with your audience also counts. You see, companies want somebody trustworthy to represent them. So, if you want to work with them, you need to have credibility and integrity. This would be great in addition to your thousands or hundreds of thousands of followers on Instagram.

Likewise, if you want your followers to remain loyal to you, you have to be selective of the brands that you work with. You must only endorse products and/or services that you truly believe in. A lot of people get turned off by influencers who trade their integrity for money and spam their content with ads. Remember that your followers expect to see high quality content from you, not promotional ads.

Furthermore, you can be part of a multilevel marketing company and build a team of online marketers. Since Instagram has millions of users, it is an ideal platform for displaying visual content. You can advertise the products and/or services of network marketers on your Instagram account. Unlike influencers, however, affiliates are typically more concerned about making sales for their partner company and earning money than generating awareness.

This moneymaking opportunity involves trackable links or promo codes that make sure that clicks get converted into sales. For example, if you are partners with a company that manufactures protein shakes and protein bars, you can post pictures of yourself drinking and eating their products along with your meals. You can also post pictures of your improved and toned physique as a result of their health and fitness products.

Of course, you should not forget to include the URLs or product links in your bio. Instagram only allows links to be posted on the bio, so you can only promote a product at a time. You can use a URL shortener such as bit.ly. Nevertheless, you may also use promo codes as your affiliate links. You can insert these codes into your posts. You should also include the contact information of the company so that your followers can contact them in case they have any questions about the products and/or services.

Chapter 11: Twitter

Twitter is another popular social media platform that you can use to make money. It is more than just a place for your rants and blurbs. You can also use it to promote your blog or website. Each time you post a tweet, you can include a detailed description and a URL link that redirects to your blog or website.

This technique works well with affiliate marketing. You can sign up with different affiliate marketing companies and select a product and/or service that you want to promote. Then, you can create blog entries and landing pages about it and make sure that all your Twitter followers see it.

Just like with other social media, earning money is not the difficult part. It is building a network and accumulating followers that you have to be strategic about. If you want to make money from social media, you need to have a huge following. As much as possible, you have to utilize a variety of techniques so that you can gain a lot of followers who can be converted into customers.

To attract the attention of people, you have to give them what they want. Aside from providing them with valuable content, you also have to reply to their tweets, follow them back, and engage with them by discussing topics, inviting them to events, or holding contests and giving away prizes.

You can also post sponsored tweets that are paid for by advertisers. Then again, you may only qualify for these tweets if you have a lot of followers. This is why building your network is important if you want to make money via social media such as Twitter. There has to be a lot of engagement going on in your account. The more followers you have, the better your chances are at getting the attention of companies and being sponsored.

Anyway, there are other ways on how you can make money via Twitter. Crowdsourcing, for instance, is another great strategy. It refers to the practice of getting contributions and ideas from a community or group. It is a tried and tested way, which has been used for years, so you can guarantee that it can help you out. You can use crowdsourcing to encourage your followers to help you fund your business or other ventures. You can turn to Kickstarter, for example.

You can also sell products. You can use Twitter as a means to send a call to action to your followers and encourage them to do business with you. Be careful not to sound too pushy. However, even if you are using modern technology to promote your business, you should still be traditional when it comes to attracting new customers and keeping old ones. Ideally, you should use tried and tested strategies such as discounts and promotional items.

You can also provide Twitter-related services. You can give your followers Twitter products that you know they like. You can offer applications that allow them to automatically generate hashtags, for example. Since there are already a lot of apps like this on the market, you should try to be more creative. Offer them something they have never seen before. Give them an app that has more functionality and is easier to use.

Searching for new leads is another option. Twitter has a superb search tool that you can use to find new customers. It can help you find them through their tweets and bios. For example, if you sell surfboards, you can search for new leads by typing keywords or key phrases that feature the word "surfboard". You will then find public tweets from Twitter users who may be interested in your merchandise. You can reply to their tweets and offer them coupon codes.

Chapter 12: Google Plus

There is another social media platform that you can use to make money – Google Plus. It is basically just like Facebook and Twitter. You can search for people to add in your circle, post status updates, upload photos, and send messages to your contacts.

The great thing about Google Plus is that it allows you to categorize your friends into different circles. You can use this feature to conveniently target different demographics. You can send messages and test your marketing messages to see which ones work best with your different circles of friends.

It is easy to set up a group on Google Plus. Just like a Facebook fan page, you can use it to send updates regarding your business. You can post news about the products or services that you offer. You can also publish reports and reviews, as well as provide information regarding discounts, promos, sales, and coupon codes.

In essence, you have to add more people into your Google Plus groups so that you can increase your chances of making money.

When you target subscribers and add more people into your list, make sure that you go for the ones who are interested. Go for people who use your services and/or products and share your updates and posts to others. Public posts are much better because they can be seen by everyone on the Internet. They bring in more traffic to your page and significantly raise your ranking.

See to it that you also include links in your posts. You can create a page on your Google Plus About section. Keep in mind that this section helps you get more clicks since it appears on your profile and standard links pages.

You should also use Google Plus Hangouts. This feature can help you meet more subscribers and interact with them on a regular basis. Interacting with these people allows you to review your developments better. It also helps you gain ideas on how you can make further improvements on your products.

Once you have created your profile, you can start creating a community. You have to include the name and details of the product in order to raise awareness and increase its impact into the community.

You should also create a cover photo. Just like in Facebook, your profile in Google Plus would look better if it has a cover photo. You have to keep in mind that humans are visual creatures. If they like what they see, they are likely to get interested and stick around. Hence, a good cover photo would make a good impression on your potential customers.

Once you have successfully created an impressive Google Plus profile, you can start marketing your goods. You can promote books, sell products, or increase affiliate products. Before you sell your products, however, see to it that you have adequate knowledge about it. If your customers inquire about its features or functionality, you should be able to provide accurate answers.

In addition, you can promote books. A lot of Google Plus users actually make money on the site by promoting and selling books. If you are an author, you can promote your own work. It is easy to spread word about your work on Google Plus since it is also easy to find groups of people who are into reading. Just add these people into your circle and spread the news.

Moreover, you can offer services. Writers, designers, consultants, and service providers use the site to promote their services. You can also start a blog that is specifically dedicated to Google Plus. You can use the social media platform to publish and share articles. Whether you believe it or not, you can actually earn $500 to $600 per month from your blog if it gets between four thousand and five thousand visits per day.

Chapter 13: LinkedIn

LinkedIn is basically the business counterpart of Facebook. This social media platform is mostly about making professional connections. It allows you to upload your curriculum vitae or résumé for potential employers to see.

You have to keep in mind that your contacts are mostly business related. So, you have to select your pictures and posts carefully. You should aim to build a professional network. You have to look professional, smart, and decent.

LinkedIn is not the right social media for your selfies and photos from parties. When you post photos or say anything about yourself, make sure that you are making a good impression on your prospective employers.

One of the best features of the site is that you can post recommendations from previous colleagues or customers about your business. These recommendations will further strengthen your claims of offering high quality products and/or services. You can post them on your business website and put a link on your LinkedIn profile.

Take note that third-party endorsements and testimonials are very important because they validate you as well as assure prospective clients that you are reliable and trustworthy. Through LinkedIn, you can build a relationship with customers and establish your brand among likeminded individuals. You may even ask your connections to help you brainstorm and come up with better marketing strategies.

Moreover, you can use LinkedIn to create groups that consist of professionals who share their ideas and thoughts with one another. In case you have any questions or you need help in finding a particular job, you can ask them about it.

LinkedIn is such a huge social networking site where professionals from various industries and sectors come together. It allows you to easily search for people who belong to certain fields and niches.

Building a network and establishing professional connections is a great way to learn from people who are older and much more experienced. Since they have been in the industry for years, you can rest assured that you will obtain valuable information. They can even be mentors who help and guide you towards success.

Anyway, you can make money on LinkedIn by marketing your business or promoting products and/or services. This is probably the main benefit of social media sites for businesses. You can also use it to give free webinars, which you can eventually monetize. Use the discussion pages to talk about your products and build your brand.

You can also use video marketing as a way to attract more clients via LinkedIn. The self-service interface of the site makes it easier and more convenient for users to upload videos. You can begin and end your video promotions anytime you want to. You may even control costs as pay per view or pay per click for prospects just like with the AdSense program of YouTube. You can also use your videos to connect your followers to your website, landing page, or blog to boost your traffic and sales.

Do not forget to utilize search engine optimization to increase your visibility on search engines. SEO helps you gain more traffic and boosts your earning potential. If you have a blog or website, you can use LinkedIn to promote it. It would be easier for you to gain traffic on your blog or website once you have built a huge following on LinkedIn. Generating lots of backlinks can help you increase your number of subscribers.

Chapter 14: YouTube

If you want to make money on YouTube, you have to think long term. You cannot become rich by uploading dozens of videos overnight. Also, you have to make sure that you produce high quality and engaging videos, including tutorials, short films, music videos, etc. Regardless of the effort involved though, YouTube is a great place to earn.

As you know, online video can change the way people view ads, brands, content, small businesses, and enterprises. This is the reason why more and more business owners and entrepreneurs are using online videos for their benefit.

According to a study conducted by the Interactive Advertising Bureau, digital video is starting to eat into television ad budgets. Two-thirds of the 300 surveyed brand marketers are switching from TV ads to online videos.

A lot of the major companies are also starting to dominate popular social media platforms such as Vimeo and YouTube. They also use Vine, Instagram, Flickr, and Facebook.

Compared to articles and audio files, videos get more views. In 2014, it was found that users played and watched videos at a 43% growth rate. It was also found that they mostly used mobile devices for viewing videos on the Internet. YouTube had the most number of unique visits at 800 million per month, making it the number one website that plays videos.

In addition, it was found that millennials are starting to switch from traditional cable companies to Hulu and Netflix. Traditional television viewing has also dropped by 17%. More and more people are turning to online videos as their means of entertainment and source of information because it is faster and more convenient.

In a United Kingdom study completed in 2013, researchers have found that people find online videos more engaging than text articles. The results stated that 39% of adults were more likely to share online videos than text articles, 36% were more likely to comment, and 56% were more likely to 'like' these videos.

Online videos are simply more engaging and entertaining. This is why a lot of brands do not think twice about spending thousands and even millions of dollars in exchange for a few seconds of SnapChat commercials.

Online videos also boost website 'stickiness'. Visitors are more likely to stay on a website that features videos. The longer these visitors stay, the higher their likelihood of buying a product featured on the site. In fact, about 40% of customers that use mobile devices claim that online videos make them want to actually buy something.

Moreover, online videos can positively affect a website's ranking on search engines. According to Forrester Research, videos are fifty-three times more likely to receive organic first-page Google rankings compared to traditional webpages. Statistics show that video results have appeared in 70% of Google's top 100 search listings in 2012.

Online videos also build trust since they allow visitors to connect with the services or products when they see them in action. According to Internet Retailer, 52% of customers claim that watching videos of products and services improves their confidence in their online purchase.

Then again, if you want to be successful in online video marketing, you may consider hiring professionals to help you with video editing and getting footage. Unless you are an expert yourself, you may want to get some help in this department.

Do not forget to include a call to action in your posts. This encourages users to check out your products and/or services. See to it that your videos are clear and direct to the point when it comes to directing your audience on what they have to do next.

Furthermore, you should not put all your eggs in one basket. This means that you should refrain from putting all your videos in just one location. As much as possible, you have to distribute them into various platforms so that they can be seen and accessed by more users. You can also use other social media sites such as Facebook, Twitter, and Instagram to promote your videos. Make sure that they are also sharable so that they can go viral online.

Chapter 15: Day Trading (FX and Stocks)

Day trading is another way on how you can make money online. However, if you are serious about being an active trader, you have to consider your options carefully.

Day trading seems like an attractive endeavor but a lot of people find it difficult. Some consider it as a dangerous game that can only be played by highly experienced investors. Hence, if you do not have much experience in day trading, you may want to practice first. Then again, you can also take risks if you want.

You can increase your chances of succeeding at day trading by increasing your knowledge on investing. You also have to invest in the right equipment. An average day trading workstation (complete with the necessary software) typically costs around fifty thousand dollars.

You have to keep in mind that speed is crucial in day trading. You must select a system that is both fast and efficient. Otherwise, you will not fare well. In addition, you have to take note that the difference of pennies per share can make a significant difference between a losing trade and making a profit.

You may also dabble in foreign exchange or forex, which is the largest and most liquid market in the world. It is actually hundreds of times larger than the stock market. The daily turnover is counted in trillions of dollars.

Forex trading is ideal for both beginners and advanced traders. It offers accessibility, liquidity, and leverage to traders. There is no need for you to spend a lot of money to start trading. You can use a small capital and begin trading currencies with a $100 deposit. The foreign exchange market is also open 24/5 – that is twenty-four hours, five days per week. It only closes on Saturdays and Sundays.

A lot of brokers do not require a deposit account for trading. So, even if you have zero funds, you can begin trading. You may be asked, however, to register for a lifetime trading account that has $25 to $50 free money. If you avail this, you will only be allowed to make a withdrawal after trading a certain volume. Nonetheless, your account will remain live during trading.

When you start trading with a broker, you may want to modify your level of leverage. Your broker should allow you to use an industry standardized procedure, select an account, and modify your leverage, which is connected to your account deposit level.

If you have just started trading, you may be tempted to buy an FX robot or Expert Adviser (EA). Some traders find robots helpful in finding out what is trending on the market. However, if you do not have sufficient experience in using them, you may have more problems than benefits. In a ranging market, for example, the robot may clear out your balance.

You can also use an online software program, which you may likewise use for online trading. Just set up an account on your computer and start trading. You can also use an automated trading software program, which allows users to automatically execute trading strategies. It's also an option to use a managed-account software program if you want to start trading without having to program the software yourself. This tool manages your account for you.

Chapter 16: E-books

Due to the advent of e-readers such as the iPad and Kindle, electronic books or e-books have gained more popularity among users. This digital format of books is less expensive and more convenient to use. Unlike a typical book, an e-book does not use ink and paper. This means less cost and space. You can download and save as many e-books as you want on your electronic device, depending on its size. With traditional books, however, you may only be able to stuff two to three in your backpack.

Users prefer e-books to actual books because of their portability. They can read an e-book on their phone or tablet while waiting in queue, travelling via train or plane, or while waiting for someone in a coffee shop. A lot of educational institutions also recommend electronic books to students so that they can experience convenience as well as adapt to modern technology better.

When you choose to make money from e-books, you will realize that the publishing process is not the difficult part, but rather the writing part. A huge problem of e-publishing is that most of their self-published books are low in quality. This is why you have to put in a lot of effort into your work so that it can be distinguished from the rest.

Before you begin writing, you have to consider if it is non-fiction or fiction that you are going to go for. You also have to determine the niche that you are going to focus on. Guides and tutorials, for example, are sought after by customers because they provide valuable and practical information. If you choose to go with fiction, what type of book are you going to write? A lot of readers like to read novels. If you go for novels, you also have to determine the genre, such as fantasy, romance, paranormal, and crime thrillers.

While it is true that the content of the book is perhaps the most important part, you should not neglect the cover. In fact, the cover of your book is also highly important since it is the first thing that customers see when they come across your book.

The appearance of your e-book cover practically determines the success of your work. This is especially true with e-books since they come in digital format and customers cannot touch them in a physical sense. When customers shop online for e-books, they can only view the image thumbnails of the cover designs. If they like what they see, they would be interested enough to click on it and get to know more about it.

As much as possible, you must use an image that ignites interest in readers. Use an image that informs them of what the book is all about. If you have skills in graphic design or photography, you can do your own cover art. However, if you do not have these skills, you can simply hire someone else to work on the design.

When you are done with the content and the cover photo, you can start to upload your book. Make sure that you also include a description that clearly explains what readers can expect. It has to be interesting enough to hook your readers, but still mysterious enough to not give away the ending or plot twists. You can include samples of your work, such as the first two paragraphs to show readers what is in store for them. If you are going to sell your e-books on Amazon, your descriptions should only be around 120 words.

Next, you have to decide on pricing. If you sell your work on Amazon, you can get 70% royalty if your book costs between $1.86 and $8.72. You can get 35% royalty if your book costs $0.94. It is advisable to keep your prices low. The less expensive your books are, the more they will sell. In the United States, you can sell your book for as low as $0.99. First-time authors are especially advised not to price their book too high.

Chapter 17: Audio Books

Today, audio books are starting to grow in popularity. They are even starting to outdo electronic books. Audio books are the recordings of materials that have been printed previously. They are especially ideal for commuters and multitaskers who want to keep up with their reading while doing other things.

You can easily make money from audio books since it is fairly inexpensive to record and distribute CDs without any copyright issues. You will not be required to pay royalties to the publisher or author.

To produce an audio book, you must select a book that was published without a copyright. Take note that most books that were published after 1920 were protected by copyright. Even their translations have copyrights. If you want to find out more details about a specific book, you can contact the United States Copyright Office.

You must also work with an audio book performer, an engineer, and a producer. The producer and engineer will help you maximize your audio book recording's production values. The audio book performer will do the voice work. Ideally, he or she should be able to do multiple voices. Performers are advised to work with vocal coaches so that they can learn how to switch between volumes and pitches as well as obtain a good sense on how to produce tension while reading.

To begin the recording session, your producer has to reserve a studio that contains all the necessary equipment for the recording of the audio book. Keep in mind that you need to produce excellent sound quality to satisfy the buyers of your audio book.

An audio book typically takes around fifteen hours to record – that is roughly equivalent to eight to twelve recording sessions. You cannot expect the performer to do the voice work in fifteen hours straight because voice tends to fade after just two to three hours.

To ensure the quality of the voice work, you have to make your performer attend rehearsals. You have to direct him or her to refine tone and pronunciation. You should be attentive in case dialogue tags have to be cut during rehearsals. There might also be other expositions.

When it comes to the recording process, the engineer has to manage studio controls while the producer has to manage the audio book's production value. On the other hand, you have to concentrate on the performer's performance. You have to review the recording to ensure that your expectations for your audio book are met.

When the recording is done and the audio book is ready, you can start distributing it to physical locations and on the Internet. You can upload audio books to music distribution sites such as iTunes. You can also turn your audio book into CD format and bring it to music stores.

Chapter 18: Apps

If you possess the right technical skills, you can develop and sell applications or apps. You can also hire someone to do the work for you. These things are excellent sources of passive income, especially since everyone is dependent on technology and mobile devices nowadays. Nearly every person owns a smartphone and has access to the Internet. It is very rare to find a person who does not use any kind of application to do tasks or communicate with others.

Another way to earn money via apps is to install and use them. Google and other huge companies pay people for installing applications. You can also get paid by simply using certain apps on your mobile device.

For example, you can instantly earn $3 when you use ShopTracker and answer several questions. If you want to keep earning $3 per month, you have to keep the app installed on your device. By answering questions, you help companies learn and understand what customers are searching for.

You can also use the Nielsen Mobile Panel. You can make up to $50 per year by using their mobile app. Moreover, you can install and use MobileXpression to get prizes every week. Simply put, if you have the willingness and patience to participate in market research, earning rewards should be effortless.

In addition, you can make money by doing tasks you found on apps. For example, you can be a driver through HopSkipDrive. You will need to have adequate caregiving experience because you will be taking care of children. You will drive them to school, to soccer practice, and to other activities. You can earn up to $30 per hour as well as take control of your schedule.

You can also use Lyft or Uber to earn money by driving. Here, you do not need to have any caregiving skills or experience. You just need to have a car and know how to drive. Your car will be inspected and you will be required to maintain a good rating.

Likewise, you can make money by being a delivery driver on Postmates. The app lets you deliver supplies and food to their clients. You can earn up to $25 per hour as well as take control of your schedule.

If you do not own a car, you can still run errands. You can complete tasks on foot via Gigwalker. The app lets you help clients who need help with errands, running events, etc. You will practically become an assistant.

TaskRabbit is an app that is just like Gigwalker. It lets you help clients by running errands or completing house projects. You can expect tasks such as wrapping gifts or moving furniture around. You can only accept tasks that you can do as well as set your rates.

Instacart is another app that you can use to earn money. It is a grocery delivery service that allows you to deliver and purchase groceries. You can choose to buy your groceries and then deliver them or you can be an in-store shopper. The latter option is preferable if you do not own a car.

If you are fond of dogs, you can walk them and make money at the same time. You can use Wag! and get paid to take pictures of dogs and basically just spend time with them.

You can also use Toot and get paid by tutoring students in various subjects, such as French and Chemistry among others. All you have to do is create a profile and wait for students to contact you. You will then have to meet them to do your job. The money you earn will be sent to you via the Toot app.

You can also be a freelancer using TisPR. This app is ideal for talented individuals who want to manage their own schedule while they earn money. You simply have to upload a profile and explain the kind of services that you provide. You will then be connected to customers in need of your services.

FieldAgent is another app that you can use to make money by completing tasks or projects that clients have started. You do not need to have a car to get to your client and do your job. Your earnings will be sent to you through PayPal. You can work during your free time or basically whenever you feel like it. The jobs are typically easy and quick. However, you may want to work on multiple jobs at the same time if you really want to make good money out of this gig.

If you're willing to offer cleaning services, you can use Handy. It is a booking app that is specifically created for home cleaning. You have to upload a profile and wait to get matched with clients who need to have their houses cleaned.

If you are tech savvy, you can try Inbox Dollars. It is an app that lets you answer surveys and play newly released games. Just like Inbox Dollars, Surveys On The Go lets you answer surveys and get paid by companies that focus on political campaigns and market research. You can earn $0.25 to $5 for every survey you complete. If you use the app daily, you can make $15 per day.

If you are a fitness enthusiast, you can earn money via Pact. It is an app that allows you to reach your fitness goals and earn money simply by working out. Furthermore, you can use Amazon's Amazon Flex. It is an app that allows you to schedule deliveries and earn $18 to $25 per hour.

Chapter 19: E-mail Marketing

With e-mail marketing, you need to have a mailing list that contains the e-mail addresses of subscribers. Keep in mind that you need to update your subscribers on a regular basis. You need to inform them about the latest happenings or breakthroughs on your website.

E-mail marketing refers to the process of making sales through e-mail. Even though it is a very old form of online marketing, it is still highly effective. To this day, people still receive e-mails from affiliate marketers to store owners offering various products and services. E-mail marketing is not spam mail. It is also not the same as pyramid marketing. It is a legitimate way to make money.

You have to keep in mind that effective and good e-mail marketing should speak to the general or specific interests of the receivers. So, when you send an e-mail to a subscriber, you have to make sure that it is interesting or helpful. You have to give your subscribers what they want. If they signed up because of hair care products, make it a point to send them e-mails regarding hair care products.

In addition, you have to keep in mind that effective and good e-mail marketing gives subscribers an option to stop receiving e-mails. So, if they no longer want to get your e-mails, they should be able to unsubscribe at any time. You should not force them to stay subscribed to your mailing list.

It is easier to personalize e-mail marketing than any other online marketing strategies. For instance, you can show the first and last names of the receivers. Also, you can use the e-mail as a direct connection between your subscribers and yourself rather than using something from your website.

Ideally, you should send personalized e-mails to your new subscribers. Each one of your subscribers should know that you are real and accessible. Also, you have to remember that your relationship with your subscribers is much more important than the size of your mailing list.

You can have a separate mailing list for every type of audience you have. Ideally, every one of your lists should be sent a separate series of e-mails. If you do it the right way, e-mail marketing can be lucrative for you. Keep in mind that your success depends on your mailing list. See to it that you make legitimate e-mail lists that consist of subscribers who wish to know more of what you say and offer.

You have to build a relationship with your subscribers if you want them to turn into customers who regularly avail of your services and products. You also have to understand that they do not want to be sold to even if they do want to buy. They will only buy from you when you prove to them that you are worth their time and attention.

Making Money from Your Mailing Lists

The following are the ways on how you can earn money through your mailing lists:

Affiliate Offers

People generally dislike affiliate offers. So, if you plan to promote affiliate products, you should avoid sending direct affiliate offers. Instead, you should do reviews on the products and upload these reviews on your website or blog. Do not forget to mention how these products help you and your business improve. Also, make sure that you include a link to your review.

Products and Services

If you're selling certain products and/or services, you can offer them to your subscribers by sending valuable content such as free reports and videos. Then, you should introduce your subscribers to your training program, products, and/or services.

Referring Subscribers

You can also make money by sending your subscribers to certain websites. There are companies that pay people to refer their subscribers to their websites and check out the offers available. You can make $1 for every subscriber that ends up downloading something from such website.

Sponsor Ads

You can include paragraphs that advertise certain sponsors to your e-mails. Make sure that you include the links to these sponsored ads. Depending on how big your mailing list is, you can earn at least $100.

Thank You Pages

Whenever new subscribers join your mailing list, you should send them thank you pages that request them to open your e-mail and verify their subscription.

Chapter 20: Stock Photos

If you like taking pictures and you have a whole stack with you, you can sell them online. If you are not really into photography but you have a collection of beautiful photos, you can also sell them on websites such as iStockPhoto and Shutterstock. You can also sign up with Fotolia, Dreamstime, and Freedigitalphotos. Selling your photos as stock photography allows you to collect payments without exerting any additional effort to market them.

It is easy to sell photos on the Internet, but you really have to be persistent if you want to make good money out of it. A lot of other people are also into selling stock photos. So, you have to do your best to outdo your competitors. See to it that you copyright your images so that other users cannot just obtain and copy them without your permission.

Stock photos are pictures that can be licensed and arranged for specific purposes. These photos are typically used by people who need them for magazines, websites, brochures, graphic designs, web designs, and other purposes. A lot of business owners prefer stock photos for their projects and advertisements because these photos allow them to save money.

By using stock photos, they no longer have to hire a photographer and spend on other related expenses. It also helps them save a lot of time since they no longer have to schedule photo shoots or have meetings with the photographer. If you sell stock photos online, you can earn a commission from the stock photography websites.

You can also choose to host a portfolio of photos on your own website and allow users to download your photos for free but restrict certain items. You can even sell advertisement space beside your photos.

If you know people or clients who are interested in stock photography, you can contact them directly and sell them your work. If they like your photos, you can create a gallery and have them as your private clients.

Likewise, if you know businesses that produce merchandise and goods such as shirts, calendars, and cups, you can offer them your photos. These photos will be printed on these items.

How Much Money You Can Make via Stock Photos

In essence, how much money you earn by selling stock photos depends on how many photos you sell and how in demand these photos are. At times, payments for every download can only give you several cents when they are sold through subscriptions. Over time, however, these prices can increase as you sell more photos. There are also websites that pay more money for photos that are downloaded frequently.

Also, you can make an arrangement with the company or website owner and tell them that they can exclusively own your photos. When you agree to these terms, your photos will be featured in their exclusive program and you can earn much more money. iStockphoto, for instance, pays three times more commissions to exclusive photographers. Dreamstime also pays bonuses to exclusive photographers.

A great thing about stock photography is that your portfolio can grow very fast and allow you to earn a passive income, even when you are not that active on the site. Your photos can stay there for years and get downloaded by thousands of online users.

However, you have to keep in mind that not all of your photos may be sold. Some of them may be rejected. Stock photography websites only accept photos that are needed or demanded by the market. So, if you want to make money from stock photography, you should submit photos that other people can use for their websites, graphics, logos, icons, and merchandise.

Also, you have to take note that stock photography websites have their own policies with regard to payment. Most of them require users to reach at least $50 or $100 before they can withdraw their earnings. You may want to read and review the guidelines and rules first before you sign up for any stock photography website.

Chapter 21: AirBnB

Frequent travelers are aware of how expensive and difficult accommodation can be. Hotels, motels, and inns are usually the options of people who need to spend the night away from home. However, these options typically cost a few hundred dollars per night, and that may not be practical for someone who is on a budget.

Because of these problems, Airbed & Breakfast or AirBnB has been born. Travelers can now enjoy the perks and privileges of being in a house with actual furniture, kitchen appliances, and a private space. They can now travel anywhere without worrying of spending too much for a hotel room.

With this being said, AirBnB seems like a really good business venture. You can offer guests quality and inexpensive accommodation, in exchange of a good feedback and loyal patronage. If your guests liked your services, they can be your regular clients every time they go out of town and stay in your area. Positive ratings can also improve your reputation and popularity.

You can rent out your entire house for the weekend or a few days. If your guests are on a vacation or an important business trip, you can choose to rent out your place longer. You can also just rent out a room if you want. Since you are just starting out, you can test the waters and sign up with AirBnB for a while. Upload your listing with the duration of just a weekend or a week. Of course, AirBnB would get a cut from your earnings.

Getting Started

It is free to sign up on AirBnB. You just have to fill out the form and provide your personal details. No need to worry about your sensitive information being leaked. AirBnB has a good privacy policy. Your listings will also be kept confidential until you are ready to get them published online. You get to choose the rates for your listings. You also get to choose the duration. If you want to attract more travelers, you can offer discounts and other perks and privileges.

Advertising space is also easy. You just have to go to Titles and Descriptions and then provide your descriptions and house rules. You also have to upload 24 or fewer photos. Ideally, you should upload as many photos as possible so that prospective clients will see what you have to offer.

Interested clients can contact AirBnB to ask about your listing. Some of the common concerns that travelers have include nearness to public transportation, tourist spots, and restaurants, as well as amenities and location. You can either approve or decline a booking proposal. You have 24 hours to contact the client and discuss his reservations. Afterwards, you can leave a review or feedback.

If it is your first time using AirBnB and you are worried about your house being trashed or damaged, the company offers an insurance policy that costs $1 million for property damage. However, this insurance does not cover normal wear and tear, personal liability, and stolen cash, artwork, and jewelry items.

Nonetheless, you may want to ask for a security deposit to cover any potential losses. A security deposit of $100 to $500 should be enough to cover any damages that your guests may incur. Make sure that you also store your personal belongings properly. You can keep them locked up in a spare room.

On Being a Good Host

Surely, if you want to be successful with your AirBnB business venture, you need to make sure that you are a good host to your guests. You would not have a hard time getting clients if you live in a huge city such as New York or Los Angeles. A lot of people go to these places for vacations and business.

Then again, you have to consider certain things that your guests may need such as a parking space, smoking area, private bathroom, and kitchen. If your house is located on a busy street, the noise outside may be bothersome for the guests. If your house is too far from the city proper, your guests may have a hard time commuting or taking public transport. You also have to consider the preferences of your guests.

You can choose to rent out your entire house or just a spare room. If you are only renting out a room, you should ask the guest if he wants to have access to the kitchen. It is also a good idea to let the guest use another bathroom for privacy and hygiene purposes. Do not forget to give tips and instructions that may be helpful to your guests. Let them know about any unsafe routes if there are any. You may also give them tips with regard to the most popular bars and restaurants, as well as the tastiest local dishes in your area.

Chapter 22: Shopify

The website Shopify is ideal for selling products. Over 70,000 users log into their accounts on a regular basis. The site is also linked to General Electric, Wikipedia, Amnesty International, Pixar, and Evernote among other major companies. You can easily set up an online store and no longer worry about hosting and domain. They also provide CMC, designs, and payment gateways for users. Shopify is an e-commerce website that you can use if you are new to online selling. It gives users a hundred professionally designed themes they can use for their stores.

Then again, you have to take note that selling on Shopify is not free of charge. Even so, it is still a much cheaper alternative to setting up your own e-commerce website. If you choose to set up your own website, you will need to spend at least $600 for themes, hosting, setup, plugins, etc. Selling on Shopify is even cheaper than selling on Amazon and eBay because you do not have to give them 10% of your sales.

If it is your first time, you can go for a basic package. Shopify will then get 1.5% from the money you make from selling. So, if you made $200 from selling a particular product, Shopify will get $3 from you. That is not such a bad price. If you are still skeptic or hesitant about the whole ordeal, you can try their fourteen-day trial for free. If you did not like your experience with Shopify, you can simply quit. They will not force you to stay. On the other hand, if you were satisfied with your experience, you can continue to sell as usual.

As you stay longer with Shopify, you become a more experienced seller. By this time, you can go for their premium package and pay $40 a month without giving them any percentage from your sales. This option is more ideal for experienced sellers who really want to make a profit from selling. You can sell as many items as you want and get to keep all the fees to yourself.

Getting started is easy. First, you have to create your Shopify account. Go to the homepage and click on the trial button. You are now ready to register. Make sure that you provide all the necessary information. Afterwards, Shopify will send you an e-mail that you need to confirm. Once you are done with that, you can log into your Shopify account with your user details and password.

When you are in, you have to click on the button that says Create an Online Store. From there, you can start to add products. It is easy and simple – the entire process should only take a couple of minutes. Then, you can select a theme for your online store as well as a custom domain. This link is where your products are going to be stored in. You also have to select the category for your products so that your store can be ranked highly on Shopify.

Do not forget to click on Submit to get started. You can now start sharing your links on social media and other platforms and earning good money. You can also offer discounts for your merchandise by sending discount codes.

Chapter 23: Answering Professional Questions

If you are an expert on a particular area, perhaps you can help other people find answers to their questions while you make money at the same time. You can go to websites such as LivePerson and Just Answer to provide answers to professional or technical questions. Of course, when you give an answer, see to it that it is correct and accurate. It also has to come from a reliable source. If you cannot cite a particular website because you are answering from experience, make sure that what you say is actually true and credible.

LivePerson is a website where people ask questions and you give them the answers that they are looking for. Just Answer is a website with more than twenty million users. When you sign up as an expert, you can earn $5 to $25 for every answer you give, provided that your answer satisfies the asker. You can withdraw your money via PayPal once it reaches $20.

You can also go to WebAnswers, which is another popular website for answers and questions. The website features ads from Google AdSense. It is practically a revenue sharing website. Any person can go to the website to answer questions and make money. If you post an answer and it gets chosen by the asker as the best answer, you will earn a revenue from Google AdSense. Your answer will also get published for other people to see.

If you want to earn more money, you can take advantage of the two Referral Programs on the website: Traffic Impressions and Referring New Users. You can earn 20% impressions from visitors who directly go to the website. You just have to apply a unique tracking token. You can also make an additional 10% on the referenced activities of the users when you make referrals.

Ether is a professional website that features experts and specialists on a variety of fields. So, if you are an expert on something, you can make money by sharing your knowledge. You can give advice through phone calls. You can also sell products to customers. Make sure that you provide your rate per minute or hour, as well as your routine schedule.

Furthermore, you can join Studentoffortune. It is a website where students and experts come together to help each other out. Students who need help with their homework or research assignment can ask professionals in exchange of an amount. This is great because you get to help students pass their subjects while you share valuable information and earn money at the same time.

Chapter 24: Online Courses

Since the start of the Internet era, nearly everything has been uploaded online. If you need to know about anything, you can try to look it up and there is a huge chance that you would find it. You can search for books, recipes, patterns, movies, etc. Educational courses are not an exception. These are commonly referred to as massive open online courses or MOOCs.

If you want to enroll in a particular course, you can choose an online course from an online learning platform such as Udemy. Take note that you may not use these courses for college credits. Nevertheless, they are still useful in improving your professional skills. They can also get you credit for technical certifications.

If you are an expert, you can develop courses and publish them online in the form of PDF, PowerPoint presentation, zip file, audio file, or video. Some of the most popular courses include those related to language, music, art, health and fitness, science and technology, and business. You can also develop academic courses if you work in the academe.

Most courses found on Udemy are priced between $29 and $99. You can earn as much as 97% of the tuition revenues depending on the strategies you use for marketing. You can earn up to $7,000 for the online courses you make. You can even make more than that depending on your popularity and skills. You can take advantage of social media platforms and boost your popularity through fan pages.

At first, you can offer your online courses for free. Free courses tend to attract students who want to learn and improve their skills without having to spend anything. If they like what you offer, they can be your followers. The next time you release your online course, they would be more likely to pay for it because they already know your style and they trust your teaching.

Aside from free online courses, you may also offer discounts. For instance, if you have a three-part course, you can offer the first one for free and then offer a discount for the second one. Students are more likely to sign up when they know that they would be eligible for a discount for your next course.

In essence, your online course can be your revenue engine as well as lead generator. Take Lili Balfour, for instance. She is a financial adviser for startup business owners. She developed six courses, including Finance Boot Camp for Entrepreneurs and How to Crowd Fund a Million Dollars. She has courses that run for only half an hour and other courses that last for two to three hours. Most of her courses are priced between $47 and $197.

The time you spend developing an online course depends on your skills and experience. At first, it may take longer for you to finish it because you are just starting to figure things out. As time passes, however, you will find it easier to finish creating a course. If you have already created a book regarding the topic, you may find it easier to turn it into an online course. You may spend two to three hours on the course.

For courses that require editing and filming, you can either do the job yourself or hire someone else to do it. Video editing is another skill required for certain online courses. If you want your course to be of high quality, you need to produce good video edits. If you do not know how to shoot videos, export them, upload them, and fix their noise, then you may want to hire a professional for the job. You may even need a crew for "talking head" style videos. In addition, you may want to consider renting a studio as well as audio and lighting equipment.

Chapter 25: Virtual Assistant

You can be a virtual assistant if you know how to use Microsoft Office programs such as Excel, PowerPoint, and Word. You also need to have good communication skills and be able to follow deadlines. Virtual assistants are freelancers who provide online support to clients by working remotely. They offer services from their home, which means that they do not physically go to the offices of their clients.

A lot of startups hire virtual assistants instead of full-time employees because it is less expensive this way. By outsourcing services, they are able to save money. In order for you to be an effective virtual assistant, you need to have administrative skills for secretarial tasks. You also need to have time management skills as well as a good command of the English language.

You can expect your job to include sorting and reading e-mails, answering phone inquiries, making follow-ups, booking tickets and appointments, managing calendar activities, updating the database, and filing.

If you work as a digital marketing virtual assistant, you have to know the ropes of online marketing. You can work as a search engine optimization assistant, a content marketing assistant, or a social media management assistant. Your job description may include analyzing data to achieve the return on investment; planning, scheduling, and managing content; making campaign strategies as well as analyzing success; and conducting competitive analysis.

If you work as a programming virtual assistant, you can work on websites or mobile apps to optimize the online presence of startups. Your tasks may include designing websites, apps, or plugin layouts; maintenance and updates; troubleshooting and debugging; uploading content; and making sure that the app or website can be searched by users easily.

If you prefer to work as a design virtual assistant, you need to have graphic design skills so that you can make the website of the company user friendly. Some of your tasks may include designing business websites and mobile apps; designing business cards and flyers; infographic designing; creating product boxes and shots; and presentation design.

You can also work as a writing virtual assistant if you have good writing skills. However, you may also be given tasks related to data entry. As a writing virtual assistant or data entry clerk, your tasks may include creating content plans, writing content with keywords, researching niche keywords, and proofreading and editing.

If you have video or audio editing skills, you can be a video or audio editing virtual assistant. Your job may require you to remove noise or apply background music. Your tasks may also include removing clutter, providing content sequences, making content visible or audible, and adding computer generated imagery (CGI) and sounds.

Furthermore, you can work as a financial virtual assistant and help business owners manage their finances. Your tasks may include documenting financial matters, analyzing account information, auditing documents, monitoring financial discrepancies, compiling liability and asset entries, and advising regarding financial management.

Chapter 26: Online Teacher/Tutor

You can also find various teaching jobs online. You can be an online teacher or tutor even if you are not a teacher or tutor by profession. Of course, you will have an edge over the others if you already have teaching experience and skills to back you up. Depending on your expertise and/or preference, you can teach language, mathematics, or any other subject.

The following are some of the websites you can go to if you want to work as an online teacher or tutor:

Udemy

The website has over ten million students. It is geared towards helping students learn through video tutorials. You can make money by creating and uploading video tutorials. You can set the price for your online courses. You can also give discounts or promotional offers to attract more students. Aside from creating and marketing your own courses, you can also make money on Udemy by promoting the courses of other people or through affiliate marketing. You can earn a commission for every purchase.

Tutorvista

The website is composed of online tutors and students from different parts of the world. You can either work full time or part time. You can also teach college or high school students. It is free to sign up. At present, there are over two thousand tutors on the site. They mostly specialize in school subjects such as English, Math, and Sciences.

Tutor

Tutor.com has over two thousand and five hundred expert teachers. It is a website that helps part-time tutors get teaching jobs online. You can be qualified as an online tutor if you specialize in Calculus, Finance, Statistics, Physics, Economics, Accounting, and Chemistry among other college subjects. You may earn between $800 and $1600 when you work part time.

Transtutors

The website has over twenty thousand tutors and two million students. It is where students find answers to academic-related questions. The website is pretty much straightforward. Online teachers can make money by answering questions. The usual rate per answer is $3.

Buddyschool

Signing up is free of charge, but you will be required to pay $10 per year if you join the site. It is easy to work online on Buddyschool. You just have to create an online tutor profile and activate it. Then, you can start setting tuition fee rates as well as edit your profile.

Chapter 27: Web Design

Web designers earn pretty well. They can earn $40,000 on average per year. If you are really skilled and talented, you can make more money. Some web designers are able to earn six figures per year. If you want to be one of them, you have to do well in business. You also have to learn how to think outside the box. You have an advantage if you are adept at HTML, CSS, PHP, and MySQL. You can enroll yourself in a class or simply take online courses. One of the best things about being a Web designer is that you can work from home.

At first, you need to find clients to work with. You have to reach out to as many people as possible so that you can market yourself more effectively. When you have a steady stream of clients, you can have a baseline income. Then again, it is still much better to have multiple clients so that you can have a stable income. This way, you will still have available projects when one or two of your clients stop working with you.

You can find clients by contacting them directly or signing up on freelance websites such as Upwork and Elance. Make sure that you have a portfolio ready so that you can show them your talents and skills. You also have to be up to date with the latest trends in technology and Web design. It is highly recommended that you keep up with the current demands of the market.

You need to have your own business cards that include your contact information and specialization. It is not expensive to have business cards printed. You can get a thousand pieces for just $25. Remember that it is not enough to just search online. You also have to do some offline searching. You can walk into office buildings and inform the staff of your services. Leave them your business cards and tell them to contact you if they ever need your services.

You can also include notes or letters to further explain your specialization. Referrals are also handy. You can ask your family and friends to refer you to prospective clients. You can give a small percentage of your earnings to those who refer you. For example, you can give them five to ten percent of your earnings for a particular project. You can also offer promo codes or ten percent off your services for a limited period of time to attract more clients.

Likewise, you could make money by selling stock graphics and templates since they are always in demand for websites. Startups usually do not have the budget for professional Web designs. So, you can reach out to startup company owners and offer them your stock graphics for only a few dollars. Stock graphics are great sources of passive income because you can keep selling them. You only have to make them once and then wait for clients to come and get them.

It is true that finding clients is time consuming. So, if you are pressed for time, you may want to consider setting up a blog and waiting for clients to come and find you. Once you finished setting up your blog, you can post articles that would attract potential clients. Easy and inexpensive advertising is possible with blogs. You can quickly attract clients who are in need of your skill sets.

Furthermore, you have to be the solution to all the problems of your clients if you want them to keep coming back to do more business with you. It can be a huge hassle to look for several Web designers, not to mention expensive. So, you should be able to offer everything the client needs and wants. You can be an expert on a particular area, but you can make more money if you are a jack of all trades. For example, other than designing websites, you should also be able to offer blogging, coding, search engine optimization, and hosting services. Clients would surely prefer the convenience.

Chapter 28: Article Writing

Article writing is another way to make money online. You can be a ghostwriter. You can also use your own name. You can write articles on a variety of topics, such as health, fitness, beauty, product reviews, fashion, etc. The Internet is part of everyday living. People from different parts of the world go online every day to search for stuff. So, you can earn a good amount of money by providing them with what they need. Of course, you have to be updated with the latest news and trends when you write about these topics.

You can work directly with a business or website owner, but searching for clients can be tedious and time consuming. So, you can just sign up for websites that hire freelance writers. You can earn a fixed amount or a specific fee for every work you produce. Ideally, you should sign up for websites that pay upfront so that you can make money continuously. The following are some of the most popular revenue-sharing websites that freelance writers go to:

Hubpages

When you sign up for the website, you can immediately upload your articles. You need to write at least seven hundred words for your article to get approved. Also, you have to make sure that it is free from spelling and grammatical errors. You also need to have a Google AdSense account. Then, you can start earning money. Writers usually get paid with $100 as minimum.

Teckler

When you sign up on the website, you can earn seventy percent of the article revenues. Aside from articles, you can also create audio files and videos. You can also upload photos and make money off them. The minimum payout is $0.50. If you want to earn more money, you should include affiliate links to your Teckler entries or Tecks.

Bubblews

The website is a combination of social networking and revenue-sharing. You can earn $0.01 each time your article is viewed and another $0.01 when it is liked, shared, or commented on. When you reach $50, you can withdraw your earnings via PayPal.

Dailytwocents

The website is just like Bubblews, but you can already withdraw your earnings once you have reached $5. However, you only get paid $0.005 for every article view. Also, the viewer should stay on the page for at least thirty seconds in order for the view to count. If you want to earn more money, you can include affiliate links to your entries as well.

ShoutMeLoud

The website is all about search engine optimization, blogging, and making money online. When you upload articles, you have to include a Google AdSense code so that you can get paid by Google AdSense on a monthly basis. The pay is not that huge. You can make about $1 to $3, but if you upload a lot of articles, your earnings can rack up.

You can also sign up for fixed rate websites such as the following:

iWriter

Every article you upload on the website can earn you $1.25 for every one hundred and fifty words. You can withdraw your earnings when you reach $20. However, you have to make sure that you meet the requirements of the clients. Otherwise, you will not get paid for your work. If the clients are not satisfied by your articles, they can either reject it outright or have you revise it.

If you want to earn more money on the website, you need to have a high rating on your profile. You can get promoted to a premium writer and earn double when you get four-star reviews on at least thirty articles. You can triple your earnings when you become an elite writer, which you can reach when you get 4.5 stars on at least thirty articles.

Textbroker

The website is only available in the United States. If you want to register, you have to submit a sample article. The staff would then review it and give you a rating that ranges from 2 to 5 stars. Depending on your rating, you may earn $0.007 to $0.05 per word. You have to earn at least $10 before you can withdraw your earnings via PayPal.

Pukitz

The website is for niche bloggers who specialize in specific niches. You need to have written at least thirty articles to join. You can earn $0.50 for every article, for every month. Your article should have at least five hundred words. Your articles, however, are only rented. Thus, you can still post them elsewhere. You just have to inform the management so that they can take your articles down.

Tuts+

If you are adept at developing apps, logos, or games, Web development, Web design, and/or coding, you can sign up and earn $50 to $250 for every full-length tutorial.

Worldstart

You can sign up for this gig if you are an expert in technology and computers. You can make money by sharing tips and tricks about Windows 8 and Microsoft Office. You can make $25 to $50 for every article. The articles are published on monthly and daily newsletters as well as blogs.

About.com

This is one of the most visited websites in the world. If you become a writer, you can earn a decent income monthly. There are so many niches you can choose from. It can be quite difficult to get on the website, but the rewards are pretty amazing.

Listverse

The website is mostly about top 10 lists. You can send a good list with 1500 words or above and earn $100. You have to fill out a form to sign up. You can withdraw your earnings via PayPal.

Chapter 29: Graphic Design

If you want to make money by doing graphic design, you can start by creating ads and logos. You can earn $4 to $20 for every design you make. The demand for graphic design is high and you can make pretty good money from it. So, in order for you to make money from graphic design, you need a website, stock photos, and Adobe Photoshop or any similar software program. The following are some of the websites you can visit to promote and sell your work:

Freelancer

If you sign up for the website, you can earn a specific rate per hour or per logo design. It is a good place for new graphic designers because the site is already loaded with prospective clients. Once you have built your reputation amongst clients, you can easily make money. You can even make $150 per hour. For logos, you can charge $20. That may seem like a pretty low price, but it is a good way to capture the attention of prospective clients.

Fiverr

It is another great website to make money online if you are good with graphic design. You just have to market your portfolio to attract prospective clients. Once you get the hang of it, you can easily sell ten to twenty logos per day. You can earn $24 per hour, selling your logos at $4 each. Of course, you can make more money if you have good reviews. (Since Fiverr isn't just a hub for graphic designers, we'll discuss it in length in a later chapter.)

48hourslogo

You can earn at least $1000 per day when you sell five to ten logos. The usual rate on the website is $99 per logo. However, you can earn more, depending on the demands or requests of the clients.

Chapter 30: Online Surveys

If you can spare a few minutes each day, you can make some extra money by answering online surveys. There are plenty of legit online survey companies you can join. Here are some of them:

Pinecone Research

The website pays $3 for every survey you complete. All you have to do is sign up for the website and you can start answering surveys right away.

MySurvey

When you sign up for the website, you can earn points and exchange them for prizes or cash. 1000 points is equivalent to $10. MySurvey is also an online survey company that pays people to answer surveys.

National Consumer Panel

Once you become a panel member, you will be given a handheld scanner that you can use to scan bar codes of purchases. You have to transmit the information you acquired to Nielsen once every week. When you do this, you get to earn points that you can exchange for items found on the Nielsen Gift Catalog. You can choose from a variety of merchandise.

Opinion Outpost

When you sign up for the website, you can get paid with rewards each time you successfully complete a survey. These rewards can be exchanged for cash, sweepstakes, or instant win opportunities. You can also test products for free and get opportunities. In addition, you can get paid with $5 in Amazon gift cards or $10 cash rewards.

Toluna

Signing up for the website is quick and easy. When you become a member, you will get 500 points instantly. These points are your welcome points. Once you have accumulated 60,000 points or more, you can start redeeming your rewards. You can exchange these points for a variety of reward items.

Inbox Dollars

You can make money by reading e-mails, answering surveys, and surfing the Internet among others. When you become a member, you can also get free gift cards.

OneOpinion

While not as well known as the other entries in this list, OneOpinion is still a good choice if you're looking to make more money. Take note though, that the best rewards (such as Visa debit cards) require at least 25,000 points. The pace at which you accumulate these points will depend on how active you want to be, as the company gives you the option to complete surveys at your own pace.

It's safe to say that answering online surveys isn't among the highest-paying gigs on the web. That's why if you see an offer that seems too good to be true or out of the norm, you should think twice before signing up. You might end up wasting your precious time on bogus posts if you're easily tempted.

Chapter 31: Swagbucks

Swagbucks is a website that is linked to a variety of companies. When you sign up for the website, you will be connected to different brands, products, and companies. You will also be rewarded every time you take part in activities. These activities include taking daily polls, using search bars, getting free samples, and watching videos among others.

You can earn 500 to 1000 Swagbucks, depending on the activities you do. You need to have at least 300 Swagbucks to redeem your gift card, which will be sent to you in seven to ten days. Aside from this, you can also make money on the website by purchasing items. The more Swagbucks you earn, the more gift cards you can have. You can use these gift cards with more than 144 stores.

The following are the activities you can do to earn Swagbucks:

Completing daily polls

You have to answer "true or false" questions. You may also encounter questions that come with several options for the answers. All you have to do is choose an answer and click on the submit button.

Completing daily NOSOs

No Obligation Special Offers, also referred to as NOSO, can be completed if you want to make money on the website. There is a different offer on every page, but you may want to check out more deals to see all the available offers. When you are done, you will need to input a CAPTCHA.

Searching

You can also use the search engine of the website to earn money. You can win by doing five searches or less. You can search for anything you usually type into the search bar. Then, you can earn seven to fifteen Swagbucks. If you do more searches, you can earn more.

Using swag codes

Swag codes are alphanumeric phrases that are issued for a limited time only. They are usually a combination of lowercase and uppercase letters that can only be seen for one to two hours. If you want to get notifications for swag codes, you can install an extension on your Web browser, follow Swagbucks on your Facebook, Instagram, and Twitter accounts, and/or read their blog. When you see a Swag code, you can copy and paste it on your Swag code box and then click on Redeem Swag code to earn some Swagbucks.

Using the Swagbucks inbox

When you join Swagbucks, you will be given an inbox in which you will directly receive special offers every single day. These offers include quizzes, polls, and surveys among others. They are not the usual offers you will find on the homepage. So, see to it that you open your inbox daily to see if you have any special offers.

Meeting daily goals

For each day, you need to meet a certain goal to earn additional Swagbucks. You can get three to ten Swagbucks, or maybe even more if you are able to meet your daily goals.

Using the mobile application on Fridays

Fridays are Mobile Swagbucks Days. This means that you can earn more Swagbucks on Friday if you use the app to search for stuff on your phone. Do not forget to share your winnings using the hashtag #MSBD as well as your Swag name. You can earn 25 Swagbucks if you get chosen.

Shopping

You can also shop using Swagbucks and get a discount or a reward. You can get four Swagbucks for every one dollar you spend at Walmart or seven Swagbucks for every one dollar you spend on Amazon.

Answering surveys

It usually takes ten to twenty minutes to finish answering surveys on Swagbucks. You can earn 75 Swagbucks for these surveys. Even if you do not qualify as a survey taker due to your location, you can still earn one Swagbucks.

Watching videos

You can watch videos for thirty seconds to a couple of minutes and earn two to four Swagbucks. You will find a meter beneath the video player. Once you have reached the required period of time for watching, which is usually about ten to twenty seconds, you can click on the next button to get your Swagbucks. In addition, you can watch sponsored videos, which are short video advertisements. You will be required to answer questions for thirty seconds to three minutes. For every video activity you complete, you will earn two Swagbucks.

Discovering special offers

You can set up a particular e-mail account for your Swagbucks offers. You can search for free offers and earn 100 to 750 Swagbucks. These special offers vary throughout the year according to season and occasion. You can expect special offers during Christmas, Valentine's Day, Mother's Day, New Year's, and other special occasions and holidays.

Playing games

You can earn ten Swagbucks when you play games on your free time. This is really a great idea because it combines fun with making money.

Chapter 32: Website Testing

You can also make money online by testing websites. Check out the following sites if you're interested in that kind of endeavor:

User Testing

You can earn $10 to $15 in twenty minutes. If you want to be a website tester, you have to apply and send your e-mail address. You also have to take and pass an exam before you can take assignments. Your earnings will be sent to you via PayPal. The tests usually last for fifteen to twenty minutes.

Enroll

If you want to enroll in this program, you have to send your e-mail address and password, and then select your method of testing. This could be with your laptop, desktop computer, smartphone, or tablet. When you are done registering, you would get e-mails that contain the assignment details. These assignments can vary, as well as your earnings. You have to use PayPal to withdraw your earnings.

StartUpLift

You can make money on the website by answering questions from various companies. These companies would also assign certain tasks that you need to complete if you want to earn $5. You can withdraw your earnings via PayPal on a weekly basis.

Testing Time

You can make money by completing studies via Skype. You can take between thirty and ninety minutes per study. When you are done with the study, you will receive your payment within five to ten days. You have to use PayPal to withdraw your earnings.

TryMyUI

You can make $10 within fifteen to twenty minutes. Once you have signed up with the website, you have to take and pass the qualification exam. This exam would determine your understanding of the processes required by the website. If you qualify, you will receive e-mails that contain details of your tasks. You have to use PayPal to withdraw your earnings on a bi-weekly basis.

Userfeel

You can earn $10 by giving your opinions and thoughts on different websites. You need to register and create an account first. Then, you have to take and pass a test. If you qualify, you will be sent e-mails that contain your assignment details. You have to use PayPal to withdraw your earnings at the end of the week.

UserZoom

You can make money by taking part in studies. The company pays $5 to $10 for every usability test for mobile and desktop platforms. Most of these tests take around ten to fifteen minutes to finish. You can get your earnings within ten to fourteen days upon completing the study.

Userlytics

You can make money by giving feedback on applications, websites, concepts, and prototypes among others. You have to register and create an account. Then, you will receive an invitation to do assignments. When you are done with these assignments, you can withdraw your earnings via PayPal. Each assignment costs $10.

Validately

You have to complete website and mobile tests for different companies. Your earnings can vary depending on the tests you do. A five-minute test, for instance, can earn you $5. Live tests that require you to share a screen or speak on the phone can give you at least $25 for half an hour. You can withdraw your earnings via PayPal within five days.

WhatUsersDo

You can make money by providing feedback on the websites of clients. You have to fill out your application and then take a test. If you qualify, you will get your assignments through e-mail. Every test takes around twenty minutes to finish and pays about $12.50. You have to use PayPal to withdraw your earnings every 25th of the month.

Chapter 33: Product Review

Doing product reviews is another way to make money online. People tend to go online to look for reviews to find out what others think of certain products, to be wary of scams, or to know if certain brands really follow through with their claims. There are also those who compare similar products based on price and reliability. Another reason why people search for product reviews is to weigh the advantages and disadvantages of certain products.

The easiest way to earn money via product reviews is to work with a company that manufactures and markets a product you prefer. You may also work with a third-party website or an online merchant. This is what is known as affiliate marketing. You get to earn a commission each time you successfully referred a customer or made a sale.

You need to sign up for an affiliate program and then promote the product. You have to use special links that track the sales so that you can get your commissions. Amazon, Linkshare, Commission Junction, and Shareasale all have affiliate programs that you can join. When you write reviews, see to it that you consider several factors.

For starters, make sure that you only write honest reviews to maintain your credibility. You must not be biased if you want your readers to trust you. You must always state the pros and cons. Keep in mind that it is not your responsibility to sell the products. The online merchant is the one responsible for that. As an affiliate, your job is to help the online merchant sell these products by promoting them through product reviews. At the same time, you should help buyers come up with intelligent decisions.

Ideally, you should try the products yourself. This way, you can really speak from experience. Some online merchants give free samples to their affiliates. However, if you do not receive any free samples, you can just buy the products. You can also read forums and blog posts for comparison and ideas from other users of the products.

The most ideal place for posting product reviews is on personal blogs or websites. You may have to spend some money on hosting and domain, but it is worth it. You may want to search for free hosting if you want to save money. However, if you do not have your own website, you can use free blogging platforms such as Blogger, Squidoo, and Hubpages. You can also post video reviews on YouTube.

Of course, if you want people to read your reviews, you have to make them presentable and organized. You need to have a title that is catchy and descriptive. Your title should give readers an idea of what your review is going to be about. You can use keywords and key phrases for search engine optimization purposes. After the title, there has to be an introduction. Your introduction should give the readers an outline of what they can expect from the review.

Then, you have to write the body of the review. It should contain all the necessary details, including the advantages and disadvantages of the products. It should also answer any potential questions that buyers may have. Finally, you need to put a recommendation. After all, your main objective is to encourage the reader to buy the product. Make sure that you give a thorough and convincing explanation on why you recommend the products.

Chapter 34: Data Entry

Data entry is another common way to make money online. It mostly requires fast typing skills. So, if you can type at least fifty words per minute, you can apply for a data entry position. Keep in mind that clients pay depending on the quality of the inputted data. Thus, you need to make sure that you only submit high quality work. Some of the tasks you may be required to do include office support, clerical work, outsourcing, research, and online marketing.

When it comes to looking for data entry jobs, make sure that you check out reviews about the available companies. Remember that there are plenty of scammers online. If you have to give them money, then it is most probably a scam. If you are required to get a subscription, make sure that you verify if they offer a money back guarantee.

You can consult the Better Business Bureau or BBB before you apply for a data entry job online. Their website features a list of the fraudulent websites that claim to offer online data entry jobs.

You may also want to do additional research by checking out forums and communicating with other people who do online jobs. You can also use search engines such as Yahoo, Bing, and Google to do a quick background check on the company. Make sure that you read the reviews carefully. Take note that some people get paid to write positive reviews. If the review sounds too good to be true, then it probably is.

In addition, you have to inquire about the services they need. Find out if you are going to be paid on a monthly or weekly basis. Before you pay for a subscription plan, you may want to test the waters first by setting up an account with a website that offers free subscriptions.

Online data entry jobs do not have a lot of requirements. You do not need to possess a particular college degree to qualify for the job. You do not even have to undergo special training. If you type fast, know how to use the computer, and are adept in the English language, you can take on an online data entry job. You may work for research companies, e-commerce stores, manufacturers, educational institutions, and book publishers among others.

The following are some websites you can check out if you want to apply for an online data entry job:

My Data Team

If you want to sign up for the website, you have to pay $49.95. After you register, you can start working right away. You are not required to have a previous experience before you are allowed to work. If you are not satisfied with their program, you can get your money back within sixty days.

Work from Home Data Entry

Before you can work, you have to undergo training, which costs $99. If you sign up for the website, you can earn several hundred dollars per day, depending on how much work you do. So, the more work you do, the more money you can make. The earnings are not fixed. If you are not satisfied with their program, you can get your money back within thirty days.

Online Data Entry Jobs

If you want to sign up for the website, you have to pay $49.95. Just like the other websites, you can start working immediately, even if you do not have any previous experience with data entry. If you are not satisfied with the program, you can get your money back within thirty days.

Chapter 35: Online Travel Agent

You can be a homebased travel agent and earn commissions from a host agency affiliation. The host agency will give you credibility and allow you to earn commissions in exchange for your services rendered. However, you need to make sure that the host agency you choose does not cheat you out of your commissions. As much as possible, you should do your research on the available host agencies.

Aside from commissions, there are other less obvious ways on how you can earn money as a homebased travel agent. Traditional travel agents typically deal with cuts, caps, and eliminations of base commissions. If you ever have to do business with airlines when you sell tickets, make sure that you can still earn money without having to depend too much on them.

For instance, you can make money by helping your clients with their hotel reservations. This is especially useful if they are traveling in a certain country where they do not speak the local dialect. If you can speak the foreign language, you can help them out and charge a fee. If you know about other charming accommodations other than popular hotels, you can recommend these places.

As an online travel agent, you can make more money if you possess specialized expertise and knowledge, which people cannot easily get from the usual store front agencies. You can even provide tips and advice to travelers with regard to the best dining places, hidden views, and other beautiful places most tourists do not know about.

You can also make money by selling high and buying low. This strategy is not really new. You have to take note that not all travel products are sold on commission basis. A lot of times, travel agents buy products at a certain price, including tours and airline tickets, and sell them at a higher price. This gives them a chance to set their own commissions. Some people refer to this strategy as the distributorship model or merchant pricing.

Take consolidator tickets, for example. If you are aware of where to get them, you can purchase a ticket for $800 and then sell it for $900, whereas airlines would sell the same ticket for $1,000. Since you only got the ticket for $800 and the customer bought it for just $900, both of you were able to benefit. You got to earn a profit while the customer got to save money.

Then again, there are more ways on how you can make money as an online travel agent. These ways are unusual, but they are profitable. For example, you can earn extra money by showcasing your specializations. You can actually make more money by selling inexpensive travel tickets and taking smaller commissions than by selling expensive travel tickets and taking bigger commissions.

Likewise, you can make more money if you know whom to sell to. For instance, you can choose to focus on customers who are on a budget. These people are always hoping for great deals and cheap travel. So, you can make them your target audience. You can offer them free sightseeing and restaurant advice or rebates when they purchase your inexpensive airline seats.

On the other hand, you can also choose to cater to people who do not mind splurging and spending a lot of money in exchange for special treatments and specializations. These people do not mind the expensive tickets and accommodation because they are after relaxation, unforgettable experiences, and fun, not staying within a certain budget.

Chapter 36: Online Games

If you love to play online games, this is great news for you: you can actually earn money just by doing your favorite hobby or pastime. The following are some of the games you can take on if you want to make money online:

Swagbucks

This online rewards program does not only give users rewards when they use the search engine. It also gives them the opportunity to make money by playing games on the site. The company is now a GPT site. As a user, you can expect arcade and word games. As you play games, you earn credits called Swagbucks. As we have previously discussed, you can exchange these Swagbucks for coupon codes, Amazon gift cards, and other cool prizes – you can even convert your game credits to cash, which you can withdraw through PayPal.

Exodus3000

This one is a highly popular multiplayer RPG strategy game. In the game, you would be sent to the future, about a thousand years from the present year. There, you will find out that the Earth is no longer an ideal place to live in because of the catastrophe that occurred. Every inhabitant has to search for Mars Dollars and minerals. Once you have reached a particular amount, you can withdraw it in real time currency. When you first sign up for the website, you will be given 5,000 Mars Dollars for free. For every 300,000 Mars Dollars you get, you can get $20.

Play Rummy

If you want to earn a really good amount of money, you should choose this one. The gaming website is especially recommended to players who are fond of playing rummy. You may also download the application from the iPhone app store and Google Play. The payouts are smooth and you can contact customer support whenever you need help or answers to questions.

Second Life

It is among the biggest and most popular online gaming websites. This social MMORPG has over two million active members. It mostly revolves around earning Linden Dollars, the currency used in the game. You can earn Linden Dollars by doing various tasks and activities, such as trading real estate, sitting on chairs, and creating visual content.

PaidGamePlayer

According to this website, they give out over $250,000 in cash daily. Here, you can find more than twenty-five online games that you can play. You can play Family Feud, Zuma, and Bejeweled against other players. The main objective of the game is for you to fight your way towards the winners' circle. For every winning you enjoy, you receive compensation. You get to have more benefits when you upgrade your membership, although that is not really required.

Team Fortress 2 and Dota 2

These games involve cosmetic items, which a lot of players are willing to pay for in real world currency. You can trade your items for actual dollars. Do not worry because this act is perfectly legal, and even encouraged.

Entropia Universe

Formerly called Project Entropia, this MMORPG is similar to Second Life in the sense that both games were created on real money economy. However, it does not solely revolve around the social world because players also get to deal with gameplay elements such as crafting, missions, and hunting among others. If you want to make money by trading the in-game currency Project Entropia Dollars with real world US dollars, the exchange rate is $1 US Dollar for every 10 Project Entropia Dollars or PED. The great thing about this game is that the middleman is eliminated. Hence, you can directly withdraw your PED into your bank account.

Chapter 37: Search Engines

You can earn about $700 per month just by evaluating search engines such as Google, Yahoo, and Bing. These search engines make use of specific algorithms to identify results. So, each time you type in a keyword or key phrase, you get a variety of relevant webpages that have already been narrowed down. You also get links to blogs and other websites.

Then again, in your years of using the Internet, you may have also noticed that the search engines are not right all the time. They can also make errors. Thus, human effort is necessary to correct these errors. Search engines have to be relevant, useful, and accurate. They can have these traits with the help of human design and input.

When you use search engines to make a profit, you become known as a search engine evaluator. Before you get hired, however, you need to take and pass a series of exams to test your knowledge and skills. You also need to undergo an interview process. When you start, you are most likely required to sign a non-disclosure agreement, which means that you cannot reveal certain information to other people.

Most companies that hire search engine evaluators pay them around $12 to $15 per hour. There are also companies that require search engine evaluators to work on specific days. Nevertheless, you still get to choose your own work hours and vacations. You have to work for a minimum number of hours in order to stay enrolled in the program, but you can always decide on when to work and take a break.

The pay is also great. Even better, you get to eliminate additional expenses such as fare or gas. You also get to benefit from continuous learning as you never stop acquiring new information. This allows you to know more about the world around you. So, if you want to work as a homebased search engine evaluator, you can check out Leapforce, Appen Butler Hill, and Lionbridge.

Chapter 38: Online Juror

Online mock jury is similar to real world jury; except that unlike in actual courts, there are no lawyers required to defend their cases in online jury. Case proceedings are also carried out by freelance workers who work from home. The online jury gives the verdict after the online hearing. The lawyers can only use the available feedback for their arguments.

If you work as an online mock juror, you will get paid to take part in online mock trials. Your odds of getting chosen generally depend on where you live, among other factors. There is no need for you to have certain skills or experiences, so you can easily become an online juror and start earning right away. The following are some of the websites you can check out if you want to work as a mock juror:

eJury

It is a highly popular online mock jury website. It is well-known for its non-discrimination nature. Anyone from all over the United States can become an online juror here. After signing up, you will be paid $5 to $10 for every case you take part in. This amount generally depends on the duration of the case. You get to earn more money if you work on longer cases. You can withdraw your earnings via PayPal.

Jury Talk

The website features legal focus groups as well as mock trials that last for a day. You can work as a research juror.

Resolution Research

The website recruits online jurors to deal with various mock trials, including cases related to educational, financial, and social aspects. Potential online jurors are screened first to see if they are qualified for the job.

Online Verdict

On this website, you can earn $20 to $60. However, you need to be an American citizen who is at least 18 years old to qualify. There aren't any restrictions involved when it comes to taking part in online mock trials. Your earnings are going to be mailed to you every month via checks.

Sign Up Direct

With this, you can earn $100 to $150 for every mock trial. You can qualify for the position of online juror if you are an American citizen who is at least 18 years old. Each online mock trial generally lasts for five to seven hours on weekdays and eight to ten hours on weekends.

Virtual Jury

The website is user-friendly and confidential. The amount of money you can earn generally depends on how many cases you can work on. Your earnings are going to be sent to you every couple of weeks via mail.

Jury Test

If you sign up for the website, you can earn $5 to $50 for every case you work on. You can even earn more money if you work on more complicated cases. Your earnings are going to be sent to you via check, but you can also withdraw them via PayPal.

Chapter 39: Freelance Transcription

General transcriptions are basically translated audio files. So, if you want to work as a freelance transcriptionist, you have to listen to audio files and type what you hear. There are various audio files that you can listen to, including business meetings, college lectures, court hearings, and even personal conversations. However, medical transcriptions are probably the most complicated ones. Most companies require their transcriptionists to present certifications or have years of experience before they get hired to provide medical transcriptions.

You can qualify for a freelance transcription job if you have a good ear and can type quickly. You also have to have the right tools, such as a computer for downloading files and doing research. Of course, you need to have a reliable and fast Internet connection as you have to receive and send audio files all the time. You may want to invest in a software program such as Express Scribe to make your job easier.

You may also use earphones or headsets to help you do your job more efficiently. Headsets are great because they enable you to block out any unnecessary disturbances and focus solely on the audio. You may also get a foot pedal to improve your speed as it allows you to start, stop, rewind, and fast forward audio files using your feet. This helps you save more time because your hands are free and you can type words as you listen to the audio.

In addition, you need to have a lot of patience since listening to various audio files and translating them into written versions can be quite tedious. You may have to listen to the audio files over and over again before you can fully decipher the message.

As a freelance transcriber, you can earn $10 to $20 per hour. If you are new to this kind of work, you may want to test the waters first or apply for companies that hire newbies. As you continue to do the work, the more you get used to it. You can get better with transcriptions over time. You just have to practice a lot and stay patient and focused.

Also, you have to take note that audio hours do not mean regular hours. You may be confused at first since you do not know much about the job yet. You have to take note that when you see an ad stating that transcribers get paid per audio hour, it does not mean that the transcribers get paid for all the hours they put into the work. It only means that the audio file lasts for a certain number of hours and that is the only duration that counts.

So, when you see an ad that says you will get paid $60 per audio hour, this means that you will get a total of $60 at the end of the project. This project, by the way, has to last for an hour. No, you will not earn $60 for every hour you work on the audio file. You can work for ten hours, but you will still earn a flat rate of $60 because that is the rate given for a one-hour project.

In the beginning, you can take projects that do not pay much. You can earn $45 to $50 per audio hour. As you gain experience and skills, however, you can increase your rate and work on projects that pay more. Aside from per hour payments, you have to take note that there are also companies that pay per page. New transcribers typically earn $1 per page.

Chapter 40: Rent Stuff Online

You know that selling items online is a pretty good way to earn money. You get to reach a wider audience when you go online than when you try to sell in your neighborhood. Then again, selling is no longer the only way to make money from your stuff. You can also rent out your personal belongings for money. What's more, you can rent out other things such as your room or car.

Renting out a bedroom in your house can be profitable, especially if you live in a city with plenty of travelers, tourists, businessmen, and students. Rental rooms are so much cheaper than hotel rooms. So, you and your client would benefit from each other. You get to earn cash while your client gets to save money. Nevertheless, you have to make sure that you still stay cautious when renting out to strangers or random people. You can use the following websites to post your listing and to find clients: HomeAway, FlipKey, HouseTrip, and Wimdu.

You can also make money by renting out a car. If you do not use your car often, you can rent it out for a day or the weekend. Just like rental rooms, rental cars are much cheaper than those coming from car rental services. You also do your clients a favor by helping them get a car right away. There is no more need for them to wait in line at the airport. You can use Lyft, Uber, and Sidecar to help you get matched with clients.

You can also rent out your surfboard, snowboard, or bicycle. Likewise, you can rent out other sports equipment. You can also rent out balls, golf clubs, pool tables, etc. A lot of people prefer to rent these things because it is much more inexpensive to rent than to buy. It is not practical to buy a new item if you are only going to use it a few times or for one day (such as if there's an event).

If you have a ton of books, you can rent them out as well. You can rent out to students or hobbyists. Renting out books is a good idea because it lets you earn a continuous profit. Books are always in demand because their content is important. Then again, you may want to stay updated and get the most recent versions with updated content. Even so, a lot of students are still probably going to rent your books anyway because it is cheaper to rent older versions.

Moreover, you can rent out your clothes and shoes. It is true that hygiene can be a concern when it comes to renting out clothing. This is why you have to make sure that they are properly cleaned before and after you rent them out. You can rent out formal dresses and evening gowns, as well as costumes and clothing for special occasions. You can also rent out your accessories and bags to match the outfits.

Chapter 41: Peer-to-Peer Lending

For the past years, peer-to-peer lending has become one of the most talked about alternatives to loans from banks and lending agencies. It refers to the practice of lending money to people without any financial intermediaries, such as banks. It allows anyone who has the funds to interact with those who need funding for personal or business needs.

A lot of people have started going for peer-to-peer lending because it offers more convenience and practicality. As a prospector, you can make a small investment in a loan profile. You get to choose the people whom you lend your money to as well as the interest rate of your loans.

The monthly payments involved in peer-to-peer lending generally yield high returns. Then again, this may still depend on the people whom you decided to invest in. This is why it is crucial for you to review the loan profiles carefully.

The main idea behind peer-to-peer lending is to help out both the lender and the borrower. It can help produce better rates than financial institutions. As a prospector, this could be a lucrative way to earn a passive income. You can earn as much as 8% to 12% in returns. You can also earn a 4.9% interest in five years or a 3.9% interest in three years.

The Peer-to-Peer Finance Association states that peer-to-peer lending has grown double in 2013, and it continues to grow to this day. People prefer the lower interest rates that peer-to-peer lending has to offer.

Then again, before you begin lending your money, you must be aware of the risks involved. In fact, these risks are so much higher than the risks involved with fixed-income securities. As a prospector, you take more risks to earn a potentially greater return.

You have to take note of the default risk. You have to realize that peer-to-peer loans are not secured. Just like unsecured loans and credit cards, they usually have a high default risk. Thus, you have to make sure that your potential returns are apt for the risk levels you take on with the loans.

You also have to keep in mind that peer-to-peer loans lack government or insurance backing. Thus, you may lose principal with your investments. Such loans are neither insured nor guaranteed. If one of your borrowers default, you will have not have anything to fall back on.

Furthermore, you have to take note of the interest rate and the liquidity risks. The Federal Reserve plans to increase market interest rates gradually. So, the borrowers may have to pay much higher interest rates. This can yield higher returns for the investors. On the other hand, this can be bad for peer-to-peer investments because such investments can be less desirable when the rates of returns on the other investments go higher faster.

With regard to liquidity, you may have a hard time unloading your peer-to-peer portfolio. This can be so much harder than unloading your shares or stocks from a major company. You cannot also merely pay withdrawal penalties and then get the principal back along with the interest. You need to use FOLIO investing and pay a transaction fee.

Chapter 42: Cash Back, Gift Cards, and Rebates

If you are fond of online shopping, you can use rebate websites to earn points, credits, and cash as you purchase your favorite items online. The following are some of the rebate websites you can visit to receive up to 70% cash back:

Swagbucks

Each time you shop at your favorite online store, you get to earn a Swagbucks point. In general, you get one point for every $0.01. If you have 100 points, you can get $1. For instance, you can get a 3% cashback at Walmart, a 4% cashback at Amazon, and an 8% cashback at Expedia.

BeFrugal

You can earn 30% cashback from over four thousand partner stores when you shop online. You can withdraw your earnings via PayPal once you have reached $25. You can also have your money sent to you by check or in the form of a gift card. One of the best things about the site is that they try to compete with their rivals. So, if you buy something on their website and you found another website that offers the same thing for a higher cashback percentage, they will try to match the offer and even add 25% to your account.

Coupon Cactus

You can earn a cashback reward per order. These cashback earnings can range between 1 and 30%. Some of them are at a flat rate of $63. After your purchase has been verified, your cashbacks would be sent to your account. You can withdraw your earnings via check or PayPal once they reached $10.

Ebates

When you sign up at EBates, you automatically get a 5% bonus. You can earn 5% to 25% cashbacks from over a thousand online stores. You just have to click on the Shop Now link when you shop and your cashbacks will be sent to your account in forty-eight hours. You can withdraw your earnings via check or PayPal, but you can also get them in the form of a gift that you can send to someone else or to charity.

Extrabux

When you sign up for the website, you get rewarded with $8 right away. You get to earn commissions for your purchases. You can earn 1% to 30% cashbacks, depending on the stores you shop from. For example, you can get 11% at Bloomingdale's or 12% at Kiehl's. You can withdraw your earnings via PayPal or check once they reached $10. You can also get them with a credit card payment that reflects on your statement or in the form of a charity donation.

Chapter 43: Junk Mail

You can make extra money simply by getting junk mail. Different companies can send you newsletters, magazine subscriptions, and catalogues. The objective of these companies is to find out how long their mailings take to reach their destinations. They also want to find out if their clients ever receive the mail they send.

Since you are receiving junk mail in exchange of money, you are called a decoy or mail decoy. Remember that a lot of people do not like to receive junk mail. This is why companies do not simply send out unwanted mail. They hire people like you to conduct their tests. You may even be pleasantly surprised to receive magazines that you like.

The payment options of these companies vary. For example, if you work with World Mail Panel, you will be given points each time you confirm getting their mail. You can exchange your points for exciting prizes or gift cards. You can also withdraw your earnings via PayPal. If you work with United States Monitor, you can earn $10 every month. You can get an additional $0.25 for every additional mail.

Some of the other companies you can consider if you want to earn money off junk mail include The Hauser Group and Small Business Knowledge Center (SBKC). When you decide that you no longer want to be a decoy or mail decoy, you can simply tell the company to stop sending you junk mail.

Conversely, you can also earn money by selling your junk mail. Small Business Knowledge Center (SBKC), for instance, buys junk mail for market research. They reward you with points for a certain amount of junk mail you send them. You can get a $20 Visa debit card when you've reached 2.000 points. Do not worry because they keep your sensitive information confidential.

Nevertheless, you should always be careful with your transactions online. You should never pay a company just to be accepted as a decoy or mail decoy. Also, you should do your research first before you give your personal details to any company. Take note that there are plenty of scammers out there and they can use your information against you.

Chapter 44: No-Risk Matched Betting

No-risk matched betting is like a legal gambling system. If you want to take part in it, you have to create an account and work with a bookmaker so that you can receive free bets. You also have to offset any possible loss. The bookmakers have to use certain terms that determine who places a bet first, etc.

If you take part in matched betting, you have to bet against or for a particular event in order for you to make money. There is no need for you to worry, however, because there is really no potential risk involved. Both of the bets cancel out each other. So, whatever result you get, you still get to win.

Anyway, if you want to come out ahead in no-risk matched betting, see to it that you are aware of the following different kinds of approach: automatic, assisted, and manual.

The automatic approach involves automatic systems that scan the market, compute the odds of betting to initial losses, and give instructions on how to place profitable bets. You can avail of software packages that can help you with matched betting. There are also websites that you can check out. They filter out the chances of losing and prevent the users from losing money. These options are truly helpful for novices who are new to matched betting.

The assisted approach involves software packages and websites that provide comparison tables of markets for users to bet on. Such provisions are also referred to as auto matchers. They are maintained by individuals who have acquired a deep understanding on the procedures of matched betting. They also give users matched betting calculators that are useful for comparison tables. You can choose from a variety of bets, time frame, bonuses, and stakes.

The manual approach involves finding offers, markets, and odds that users can use to odd themselves as they make useful calculations. You have to keep in mind that matching the right odds can be quite time consuming. It also requires a high numeracy level as well as a good understanding of placing bets.

Chapter 45: Clickworker

At Clickworker, you will get paid by doing micro jobs, including categorizing photos, recording phrases, and providing opinions on websites. You can also make money by completing assessments and referring other people to the site.

Just like networking sites, you get to earn money when your referrals earn money. For every payment they receive, you get to have a bonus or a percentage of their income. This is great if you know a lot of people or you are popular on social media.

You can promote the site and encourage others to join. The more people sign up for the website through your referrals, the more money you can earn. You can even encourage them to attract more people into signing up for the website. You can also share links on your personal blog or social media account.

You can withdraw your earnings via PayPal or have them sent directly to your bank account. If you choose to get your earnings via PayPal, you can expect them to be sent to you once a week. On the other hand, if you prefer to get your payments via bank transfer, you can expect them to arrive once a month.

Chapter 46: Fiverr

The website is one of the biggest providers of online-based products and services. You can work on Fiverr if you have professional experience related to accounting, graphic design, Web development, search engine optimization, or social media marketing. If you sign up, you can earn at least $5 per project. The following are some of the ways on how you can earn money on the site:

Written reports or electronic books

A lot of the jobs require customization. Thus, you need to follow the instructions of the client and produce new materials. However, you can also write a report or e-book instead of producing new materials every time. This still lets you earn $5 for every order. You can sell your work as many times as you want, provided that you clearly indicate that you are not selling the resale rights to it and that you still own the copyright.

Social media services

Many of the services offered on the site also involve social media promotions that aim to drive traffic to certain websites. You can find ones from Facebook, Google Plus, and Twitter. These promotions typically cost $5.

Writings

If you can write quickly, such as four hundred words in twelve minutes at most, you can earn handsomely. You can earn $25 for every hour you work here. Then again, even if you write quickly, you still have to make sure that you produce good quality output.

Marketing software

You can promote the websites of clients with the use of traffic generation software. You can actually earn $5 in just one minute. This means that you can earn roughly $300 per hour.

Research projects

You can also make money by using Google to produce research projects. See to it that your focus is good so that you can easily finish doing your research.

Virtual assistance

Depending on where you live, you can make money by becoming a virtual assistant. You simply have to dedicate one to two hours of your time to earn money.

Altered pictures

You can also earn money on the site by editing pictures using software programs like Photoshop. A lot of clients are always in search of people who can edit, crop, or improve their photos.

Business cards

If you have skills in graphic design, you can create business cards for clients.

Pictures with signs

This is perhaps the easiest way to make money on the site. All you have to do is take a picture of yourself as you hold a sign beside a landmark in your city.

Flyers

Once again, this is a great opportunity if you have skills in graphic design. You can make money by designing flyers for clients.

Reviews

You can write reviews on certain products and services to earn money. Ideally, you should be able to write four hundred words in a maximum of twelve minutes.

Video testimonials

You can make money by creating videos of yourself speaking in front of the camera. These video testimonials are actually among the most sought after projects of clients.

SEO-related software

Search engine optimization or SEO is crucial in online businesses. You can earn money on the site by using software programs that allow you to search for SEO keywords as well as produce SEO diagnostic results. Clients may ask you to find out the health of a website as well as which keywords and key phrases are most popular among users.

Chapter 47: Music Review

If you love music, you can make a profit by listening to it and submitting reviews. Your reviews and feedback are valuable to new musicians who want to know how they test out to different audiences. The following are some of the websites you can go to get paid by listening and reviewing music:

HitPredictor

When you sign up with the website, you can get points as rewards. You can then exchange these points for items such as headphones and CDs. You can also use your points as raffle entries. You can win $100-gift cards on Amazon among other cool prizes.

SliceThePie

It is another website you can go to review music and make money. The website especially focuses on unsigned singers. The feedback from users like you can help them find out which songs are most ideal for radio placement and A&R opportunities. You should write good, honest, and detailed reviews to boost your ranking on the website. The higher your ranking is, the more money you can earn. In general, the website pays $0.02 to $0.20 for every music review. You can withdraw your earnings via PayPal once you have reached $10.

MusicXRay

The website features a good selection of genres, so you can choose a type that suits you best. There is classical, country, pop, rhythm and blues, alternative, rock, and rap among others. When you sign up for the website, you will be asked about your favorite music and you will be given songs to listen to. You can earn $0.05 to $1 for every review you make. You can withdraw your earnings once you reached $20.

Radio Loyalty

You can earn money on the site by listening to online radio. You have to search for a radio station that plays your kind of music. You can earn $0.03 for every ten minutes you spend listening to the song or music. To ensure that you are truly listening, you will be required to input a code every thirty minutes. You can make more money when you refer other people to the website.

SongPeople

All you have to do to earn money on the site is listen to music and provide feedback for the artist. Each time you do a review, you earn points. You can exchange these points for gift cards on Amazon.

Fusion Cash

The website pays users to listen to music, watch videos, take offers, answer surveys, and refer friends among others. You can earn $25, which you can get via check, PayPal, or direct deposit.

Earnably

In terms of what you will be asked to do, this is practically identical to Fusion Cash. You can earn at least $2, which you can get via PayPal or Amazon.

Chapter 48: Selling Notes and Lesson Plans

Many college students have started selling notes to make extra money while in school. If you are a college student, you can sell your notes to fellow students for a price. In fact, several students have already turned this trade into a full-blown business venture.

Tom Brady, a senior at Florida State University, has capitalized on the phenomenon. He helped started moolaguides.com, which is like eBay for college students who need study guides and notes. He has already earned $200,000 from the business venture and expects to earn more. He sells study guides and notes for $8. Another student named Angel Card made money by selling class notes. She sold study guides for $5. By the end of a semester, she already earned $700.

You can also check out Luvo, which is an online marketplace based in Boston. Here, you will find tutoring and study materials. Many students turn to the site for last-minute notes and lecture courses. A lot of students also prefer to buy study guides and notes because they feel that they lack help from their professors. Companies such as Nexus and Course Hero also offer similar services.

Then again, students are not the only ones who make a profit by selling study guides and notes. Teachers are also making money online by selling their lesson plans. TeachersPayTeachers.com is one of the websites where teachers go to do business with other teachers. Aside from offering lesson plans, you can also make a profit by selling other teaching materials.

When you sign up with TeachersPayTeachers.com, you can choose from their free and premium membership offers. You can use the free version to try it out. If you liked your trial period, you can upgrade to the premium version for $59.95 per year. For every sale you make, the website takes 40% of commissions. If you are a premium member, however, it only takes 15% of commissions for your lesson plans and other related teaching materials.

Sharing and selling your lesson plans can be helpful to other teachers who need assistance. This allows them to save more time and energy while still being able to provide quality education to their students.

Chapter 49: Buy and Sell Domain Names

You can buy and sell domains for a profit. However, you have to learn that it is an active process, so you have to allot time and energy for it. If you cannot get buyers, you have to actively seek them out. Also, you have to be aware of the right opportunities. As a domain flipper, you have to keep in mind that once you purchase a domain, it is already a hot property. This means that you have to know when it is time to seal the deal. You also need to possess good networking, research, and negotiation skills along with adequate knowledge in marketing.

When it comes to domain flipping, you have to use the right strategies to be successful. It is never a good idea to base your strategies on your assumptions. Likewise, you should not assume that spending a ton of money on certain domains guarantees success. Each domain name has characteristics that pique the interest of different types of buyers.

In addition, you have to keep in mind that domain flipping is not that easy. You have to spend adequate time learning the ropes. You must spend at least one year learning how to sell domains. At first, you may experience failures. You may even lose money on some domain names as well as miss out on good deals. However, you will eventually get used to the business and you will get better at it. As they say, before you can be a pro, you have to be a novice.

Do not lose hope on getting good domain names. You should remind yourself that there are still plenty of good domain names out there. Even though most .com domain names have already been registered, you will still find ones that are not yet taken. If you want to be successful in this venture, you should always be optimistic. Be creative and use keywords. Many of the most popular domain names incorporate keywords and key phrases.

Moreover, you have to remember that .com does not necessarily beat other domain names. Just because you are using .com does not mean that you can rank higher than those who are using .net or other domain names. If you want to find out more about these domain names and their prices, you can search private seller portfolios and websites such as Flippa.com and GoDaddy. You can also check out Name.com, Domain.com, and Namecheap.

With regard to what is ethical and not, you have to know that squatting or registering domains is not unethical at all. Even if major companies disapprove of domain flipping, this should not deter you from doing it. Domain flipping is perfectly legal. There is nothing wrong with buying domain names and then selling them to others.

As for social profiles, you should get rid of your fear of them replacing domain names. Even if a lot of startups and online businesses prefer to use social media to interact with their target audiences, a lot of people still continue to rely on domain names. Social media platforms are not enough to be successful in business.

So, what are the steps in domain flipping? First of all, you have to determine your budget and stick to it. You can start with a small amount. Next, you have to select a good niche that can generate profits. It is crucial to find a niche that works for you so that you can keep capturing the interest of buyers. Make sure that you also take note of the most sought after keywords and key phrases.

You must focus more on the local domain names because they are more useful with local search engine optimization. You should also look for existing domain names that already have good backlinks, traffic, and Google ranking. You have to look for relevant domain names as well as consider alternatives. You must also continue searching for domain names that are not yet registered as well as domain names that have a good page ranking.

Of course, you should create a good domain portfolio, use various sales strategies to find out which ones work well for you, and calculate the risks involved. When it comes to domain flipping, you must be aware of the three types of risks, which are subjectivity, legality, and liquidity. You must also be prepared for any legal issues that may come up.

Chapter 50: Multilevel Marketing

Multilevel marketing, also referred to as MLM, involves networks of independent distributors who directly sell products to customers. Two of the most popular MLM ventures are Mary K Cosmetics and Avon. When you become a distributor, you can make money by recruiting other people and selling products. You will earn a commission every time someone from your downline makes a sale.

Then again, before you join any MLM venture, see to it that the company you join is legit and stable. You must do your research to avoid possible problems in the future. Find out if the company has already had at least five years in business. It's somewhat risky to work with a newly established company. You should also go for a publicly-traded firm so that you can assess their financial condition easily. Unlike these public companies, private companies are not required to disclose financial information.

Make sure that you verify the integrity of the management. Find out who the CEO is and learn about his background and experience. You can look at the official website of the company or do further investigation online and offline. Make sure that you are not being victimized by a pyramid scheme.

In addition, you should consider the products involved. Find out if they are of high quality and truly effective. You should also go for products that are unique and in demand. It is ideal to go for products and services that customers continually need. It is not advisable to market trendy items that will eventually go out of style. Furthermore, make sure that you only endorse and sell products that you actually believe in.

Do not forget to research about the compensation plan. You have to know how you are going to get paid. You can ask about the percentage of sales given to distributors. You can also ask about the distributions between new and old members. As much as possible, you must familiarize yourself with the various types of compensation plans.

You can also inquire about trainings and mentorship programs. You can ask about the duration of the training too. It is advisable that you do research on the business systems of the company. You must also be able to contact your superiors in case you need help or advice. If you want to be successful, you have to study the strategies of your mentors and try to adopt them.

When it comes to selling products, you can attract more prospective customers by hosting events and parties, as well as attending trade shows. The more people you interact with, the more prospective customers you can get. You can also give away promotional items to pique the interest of people. Remember that people like freebies. You can also send greeting cards and be a speaker at business and social events.

Moreover, you should definitely use social media to your advantage. You can set up a YouTube channel and upload videos that would appeal to your target market. You can create video tutorials or product reviews. You can also write blog posts and share content on Facebook. Social media platforms are effective means for promoting your products since a lot of people log into their accounts on a daily basis.

As for your downlines, you can build a huge network of distributors by recruiting your colleagues, friends, and family members. You can also reach out to strangers and people who might be interested in MLM. Make sure that you talk to the top earners of your network so that you can learn about their effective recruitment techniques. Whenever you recruit new members, make it a point to give them sufficient support.

Chapter 51: Online Translator

If you are bilingual or multilingual, you can make money online by being a translator. You will be surprised to find out how many people are in need of translators to help them write letters, translate documents, and do other tasks. The following are some of the websites you can use to work as an online translator:

TranslatorsCafe

The website is highly popular among online translators. You can upload your portfolio and set your rates for your clients. Make sure that you give a detailed description of your skills and services offered. You can offer editing, localization, interpreting, transcriptions, and subtitling, for instance. You can work for individual clients or companies and agencies. Afterwards, you can give them your rating or feedback. If you want to enjoy more perks and privileges on the site, you can upgrade your membership for $40 for three months. You can also upgrade for $70 for six months or $110 for twelve months.

Transperfect Translations

The agency is based in New York. It also has seventy-five subsidiaries all over the world. You can earn money by offering localizations, translations, and other language services. You can actually work full-time here. Your payments will be sent to you via check or PayPal. However, you need to make sure that you can meet deadlines because this agency is pretty strict.

Gengo

After you sign up on the website, you have to take and pass a translation exam for the language combination that you chose. Then, you have to wait a while for your exam to be reviewed. If you qualify, you can start working as an online translator right away. You can earn $0.03 for every word you translate. The longer you stay with the agency, the greater your chances are for being promoted from Standard to Pro. When you become a Pro translator, you can get higher-paying assignments, which are usually proofreading jobs.

Capita Translation and Interpreting

This huge agency is originally from Great Britain. If you qualify to work for them, you can get jobs on a regular basis. You can work as a freelance translator and take control of your schedule.

Protranslating

This international translation agency is based in Florida. If you qualify to work for them, you can expect a consistent work flow. You will also undergo personalized training to better enhance your performance. There is no need for you to buy your own software program since you would be using their software anyway.

Conclusion

Thanks for reading this book. Hopefully, it gave you all sorts of valuable insights on the various ways of earning money online.

Remember that there are lots of moneymaking options available to you – regardless of whether you prefer to earn actively, semi-passively, or passively. The next step is to get up and come up with a plan on how you can finally start earning through the web.

Best of luck in your new moneymaking pursuit!